LOVE × STYLE × LIFE

GARANCE DORÉ

SPIEGEL & GRAU

NEW YORK

A Spiegel & Grau Trade Paperback Original

Published in the United States by Spiegel & Grau,
an imprint of Random House, a division of
Penguin Random House LLC, New York.

SPIEGEL & GRAU and the HOUSE colophon are
registered trademarks of Penguin Random House LLC.

LIBRARY OF CONGRESS CATALOGING-IN-PUBLICATION DATA
Doré, Garance.
Love style life / Garance Doré.
pages cm
ISBN 978-0-8129-9637-1
eBook ISBN 978-0-8129-9638-8
1. Fashion. 2. Fashion—France—Paris. 3. Fashion—New York (State)—New York.
4. Lifestyles. 5. Doré, Garance. 6. Doré, Garance—Philosophy. 7. Image consultants—Biography.
8. Fashion designers—Interviews. I. Title.
TT507.D59 2015
746.9'2—dc23   2015008139

Printed in China on acid-free paper

spiegelandgrau.com

4 6 8 9 7 5 3

Book design by Elina Asanti / NR2154

To Tahmanent, my grandma.
Mina, you are forever in my heart, and I miss you every day.
And to all your beautiful sons and daughters,
who fill the world with a special kind of love, warmth, and humor
that knows no boundaries or religions.

CONTENTS

VIII
INTRODUCTION

Style

6
Story of My Style

16
LESSON LEARNED
The Scarf

18
How to Find Your Style

24
LESSON LEARNED
The Heels

27
The French Woman
Says No

34
LESSON LEARNED
The Clutch

37
Mix High and Low

41
It's Okay to
Break the Rules

44
The Tux

68
ON STYLE
Emmanuelle Alt

70
PARIS VS. NEW YORK
Life of the Party

Métier

78
The 10 Steps

91
At the Shows

100
24 Hours in the Life of
Garance Doré
Freelancer, Entrepreneur,
Boss

108
ON CAREER
Diane von Furstenberg

110
PARIS VS. NEW YORK
Things New Yorkers Do

Beauty

119
Growing Beautiful

122
The Mirror

125
How to Look Better
in a Photo

131
Long Story Short:
My Hair

146
Mani! Pedi! Facial!

151
Story of My ~~Life~~ Body

167
The Turn of the Screw
(Turning 40)

170
ON BEAUTY
Drew Barrymore

172
PARIS VS. NEW YORK
Things Parisians Do

Elegance

183
Élégance de Cœur

186
How to Not Fuck Up
Your Hello

190
The Thank-You Note:
A Competitive Sport

194
E-Mail Made Me
a Bad Person

198
Netiquette

202
Elegance Is Not…

206
Elegance Is…

208
ON ELEGANCE
Jenna Lyons

210
PARIS VS. NEW YORK
Perfection

Love

220
The L Word

224
In the Family

228
L'Amitié

232
100 Love Lessons

257
CONCLUSION

259
ACKNOWLEDGMENTS

_We're_ Connected

_I've been sharing my thoughts on life, love,
and style for almost ten years now, which makes me:_

1. A complete over-sharer.
2. A pretty seasoned opinion-giver.
3. Well, it should have made me super stylish.

So why did I pick this stupid pair of shoes this morning?

On my blog I've talked about matters so light (do I really need a pair of kitten heels?) that they evaporated an hour after being published, and subjects so deep (burying my grandmother in Morocco) that I still receive incredibly heartfelt letters about them to this day. I've written about things so embarrassing they made me want to melt into the floor, and I've also written of my proudest moments.

Sharing my stories came to me pretty late in life, but the day I got the hang of it, I began to understand the incredible power of letting your guard down, even with people you barely know.

Because when you open yourself, people will magically open up to you.

My blog began quite practically, as a way to share my illustrations. But I soon realized that what I really wanted was to start a conversation, just to see if there were other crazies like me out there. As it turns out, there were.

I embarked on a quest to capture the true essence of style. My journey took me from Corsica to the South of France to Paris to New York, and many places in between. And as I've come to learn, "style" is about so much more than the clothes we wear. It's the way we walk, the way we smile, the sparkle in our eyes, the way we live our lives. Style is a universal language, and it has the power to connect us.

I grew up in a tiny beach town in Ajaccio, Corsica, but my heart belongs to Paris and New York, my two adopted home cities. Two cities that are both so fascinating and inspiring, so similar and yet so different. I could devote an entire book to comparing their quirks and assets. and how I've tried to take the best of each for myself. Trying to hold onto my French-ness by celebrating my imperfections and savoring my daily glass of red wine, while embracing that wonderful, empowering New York swagger. Being a French woman with an incorrigible sense of irony—but also letting myself get taken by the American dream. And realizing along the way that no matter what city we're in, we all want the same thing.

We want love. We want to feel beautiful. We want to be good friends, good partners, good sisters, good daughters. We want to know how to never buy the wrong pair of shoes again. (Sorry to inform you, but you will keep making shoe mistakes until the day you die. So celebrate being alive right now!) We want to feel fulfilled by the work that we do, whatever that work may be.

Most of all, we want to find our place in this world.

And to be very stylish along the way, of course.

I found my place in this world almost by accident—more on that later—and it took me where I'd never dared to dream. How on earth do you provoke this sort of beautiful accident?

That's what I want to share with you in this book. And I hope that my story inspires you to create your own series of beautiful little accidents—and to enjoy the ride, that's what life is all about. ✗

LOVE × STYLE × LIFE

I know no~~~~
can really em~~~~

make anyone fe~~~~

and that misse~~~~

not the *end* of th~~~~

...shion and beautiful— ...s are ...e world.

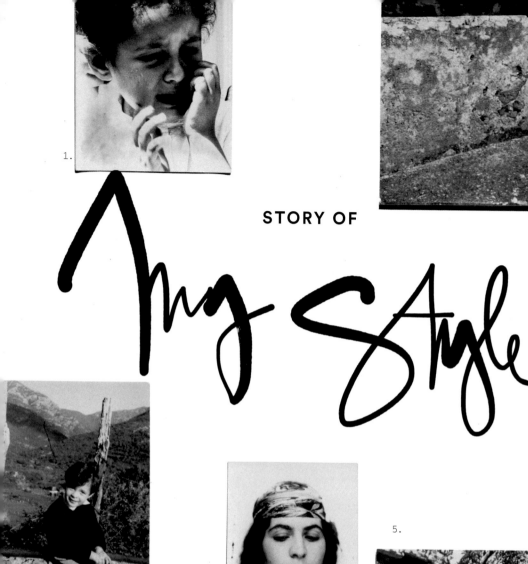

STORY OF

My Style

5.

7.   6.

1. My sister Laetitia.   2. My mother, Kheira, had a very unique sense of style.   3. My grandma, Marie, on my father's side was Italian and extremely chic.   4. My Grandma Marie and my dad, Louis.   5. Mom and me. I wish she had kept that sweater.   6. My grandma, Tahmanent, in traditional Berber dress.   7. That's me. At 8 I asked my mom to cut off all my hair. I wanted to be a boy!

2.

3.

4.

I'M 4 AND MY STYLE BELONGS TO MAMAN.

My mother, Kheira, has the most unexpected sense of style.

I don't know where she got it—maybe from my grandma Tahmanent, who was a Berber from the Moroccan mountains. My grandmother always dressed in bold colors and prints, bright frocks that complemented her long red henna-tinted hair. She loved dressing up, but she had to work within the strict codes that were imposed on her. Don't show a lot of skin; play humble.

My mother is the opposite. She's a free, modern woman and she wants the world to know. She wears tight jeans and irons her hair, and every outfit is perfectly thought out. When she has money, she buys the best pieces from Alaïa, Montana, and Thierry Mugler (hello, '80s!), and when she doesn't, she plays around with what she already has, goes thrift shopping, recuts her clothes, and gets super creative.

She wraps my head in leopard-print scarves and mismatches her stripes with my polka dots. I have to wear special shoes to reeducate my feet and save them from being flat. Instead of hiding the shoes, she puts me in light dresses to balance the heaviness with softness.

And just like that, I'm the most stylish kid in town.

But I really don't care, because before long . . .

I AM 8 YEARS OLD AND IN LOVE WITH PAPA.

I'm a daddy's girl. I love him like there is no tomorrow, and even if it will cost me a lot of money in therapy later on, for the moment all I want is the privilege of spending as much time with him as possible. So I become interested in everything he is into: cars, bikes, kitchen equipment (my dad is a chef).

He's a handsome Corsican Italian man with a very precise sense of style. We talk; he tells me about his tastes. I totally get it!

I throw all my dresses away. Dresses are for little girls, anyway.

And, I'm not a girly girl. I'm a big fan of George, the tomboy heroine from *The Famous Five,* a series of kids' books I'm addicted to. George is that daring, andro-gynous, cool- before-cool-even-existed heroine. She's smarter than all the boys and I totally identify with her—so I ask my mom to cut my hair exactly like hers.

My mom isn't afraid of my creativity (yet). She goes ahead and cuts.

I'm the only girl at school with short hair.

The perfectly braided girls in my class look at me with a raised brow and a pinched mouth. I learn what it means to be different. I don't hate it.

I AM 13 AND I'M IN LOVE WITH MARCEL.

Marcel is the most handsome skater in middle school, and I'm an extremely shy nerd hiding her newly acquired curves (read: boob explosion!!!) under huge sweaters. Of course, he has no idea I exist.

I want him to notice me. I guess I already believe in the higher powers of fashion, because I tell myself that the best thing to do is:

× *a.* Copy his style. Skater boy. Baggy jeans. Baggy T-shirts. Chuck Taylors.

Result: nothing. He still has no clue I exist.

× *b.* Refine my approach. I notice that all of Marcel's skater friends have super-girly girlfriends.

Of course—guys prefer real girls!!! Shift in strategy. I become super girly. I put on jewelry for the first time (from my mom's closet), I throw away my backpack and buy a very unpractical purse (I now have to carry my school books in my arms, like in the movies, which I feel is the epitome of chic), and I wear a fitted top, which I'm totally insecure about, but I'm ready to risk it all for Marcel.

Result: nothing. He still doesn't know I exist.

Conclusion: you don't attract guys with style. This is a very freeing insight.

Proof? The moment I figure it out, I meet my first love, a skateboarder. No, not Marcel. Marcel, to this day, still doesn't know I exist.

1.

2.

3.

4.

6.

5.

1. My grandma had a thing for scarves. 2. I'm about 10 here and my hair is growing back.
3. My father when he was a kid.
4. *The Famous Five* were my favorite books from my childhood. George was my idol! 5. About 12, becoming a teenager. 6. My father in his twenties. He is still biking today!

BIBLIOTHÈQUE ROSE

ENID BLYTON

le club des 5
joue et gagne

LE CLUB DES CINQ

I AM 15 AND IN LOVE WITH REI KAWAKUBO.

Whom I encountered through The Face, *the wonderful '90s British fashion magazine. To this day I still thank the fashion gods for the British tourists who left a copy in my dad's restaurant.*

I get a subscription and *The Face* becomes my bible. I want to be part of this world and, as you know by now, for me that translates into wanting to adopt its style.

But, my parents are not crazy about spending their money on anything that's not directly related to my education. My wardrobe allowance is below sea level, so I go on secret missions into my mother's closet.

With the help of a big pair of my dad's kitchen scissors, I turn some of her most beautiful clothes into what, in my teenage mind, resembles Comme des Garçons.

In Ajaccio, no one understands my style. *Les ignorants.*

As for my mother, she discovers my closet-plundering when she reaches for her Montana coat and finds only a single sleeve I forgot to hide in its place.

She shouts. And then she faints. And when she wakes up she locks me out of her closet for the unforeseen future.

I run off in tears, proclaiming that one day Rei Kawakubo will adopt me and everyone will finally be happy, since no one in our family understands me.

In other words, I am a teenager.

I AM 18, A STUDENT, AND IN LOVE WITH MY BEST FRIEND.

I move to the South of France to study. I am supposed to live in a dorm, but my best friend's apartment is so much nicer that we decide to live together. We study literature, but we're mostly interested in experiencing life and discovering who we are.

And by that I mean partying, of course. What's more important when you're eighteen?

My friend Anne is the best thing that ever happened to me. We understand each other without talking, but we still talk 24/7.

Our style? Agnès B. tight jeans (skinny stretchy jeans hadn't been born yet. I know, prehistoric), Agnès B. big sweaters, Doc Martens. Always the same, always matching, every day, all the time. Our dresser? Shared. Our friends? Shared. Our favorite movies? Shared. Our personality? Wait, what did you say? Our what?

Years later I discover that her feet were actually three sizes smaller than mine, but she never said anything about it, just because she was so happy to be able to share closets and Doc Martens. We had Doc Martens in every color of the rainbow, even the gold ones that are so difficult to find.

Ah, friendship rocks!!!

1. A shirt from Agnès B — I would spend all my money there. 2. Björk, my style idol when I was 20. 3. *The Face*, the magazine that opened a new world to me.

I AM 22 YEARS OLD AND IN LOVE WITH BJÖRK.

Hiking shoes like Björk, miniskirt like Björk, hair in multi-buns like Björk, and a military parka because, unlike Björk, I can't afford a coat from Hussein Chalayan.

One day, on a trip to Washington, DC, to visit a friend who lives with a colorful bunch of punk rockers, I'm feeling very free and inspired. And so, just to see what it would be like, I go to a local salon and get my head shaved.

It feels weird and amazing. More spectacular than beautiful, but I don't care about looking good. I'm much deeper than that. I'm a punk intellectual!

No, really. Shaving my head is about saying . . . It's about saying, hmmmm . . . Well, it must be saying something. Maybe just that I feel liberated by this wonderful and faraway country where no one judges me and where I can walk around with a shaved head and a coffee in a to-go cup, the most fashionable accessory there is for a French girl like me.

I AM 24 AND I'M IN LOVE WITH ROCK 'N' ROLL.

I'm into the indie-rock scene. Instead of studying, I organize concerts with a friend, having bands we love come play in our city. We book groups like Cat Power, Blonde Redhead, and—a little more cerebral, because we're deep—Tortoise.

My friends and I, we're really the cool bunch.

Again, I'm in skinny jeans (still can't find them back then, takes forever in vintage shops, but, hey, between two rock concerts and skipping class, I have aaall the time in the world), pointy flats (you can't find them back then, takes forever in vintage shops, but, hey, between two rock concerts and skipping class, I have aaall the time in the world), vintage fur (so easy to find in vintage shops, pfffff, annoying), I have a cigarette in one hand, a beer in the other, and a backstage pass around my neck.

I don't have any money—it's not like organizing concerts will really make you any, and, anyway, I'd rather spend it on beer than on clothes. So it's thrift shop all the way to achieve that look, which in retrospect was very Margot Tenenbaum. My closet may or may not smell like a vintage store, but I look cool and I'm having so much fun!

After a while, I realize that I stink, that I don't like beer, and that you can see the concert better if you're in the audience. I throw the lifestyle away, but I keep the skinny jeans and the ballet flats.

This turns out to be my first lesson in classic French style: When something works, stick with it.

I AM 26 AND IN LOVE WITH ZARA.

I'm a working girl!!! Well, I'm working but I'm still poor. After university, I get myself a job in a very stylish art-and-essay cinema, helping with press and curation. I watch movies all day; it's romantic; I'm learning so much. But I have to look good to do my job, and I really can't afford it.

That's the moment Zara opens in my city, Marseille. Life revolution. I fall in love with the prices and the fact that suddenly all trends are available to me. Goodbye, thrift stores! No need to look like a dusty library rat anymore. Shiny new clothes—bring it on!

In the span of a few months, my wardrobe is 80 percent Zara. Zara becomes my religion, and I make sure to go to my church once a week in case a fashion miracle has happened. And Zara delivers: Fashion miracles always happen there. Soon I have no idea how I ever got dressed in the morning before Zara.

Problem? Same look as all my friends. No, wait . . . Same look as my entire city. No. Same look as all of France! No. Same look as the entire world!

Looking like everyone is looking like no one, I tell myself while taking a drag on my cigarette.

I go back to my thrift stores and learn to mix it up. By that time I have a proper washing machine and I know which fibers and fabrics to avoid. Tergal, get out of my way. You stink!

I even learn how to iron. I'm an adult. I know things. Sort of.

I AM 27 AND I AM SUPER EXTRA BROKE.

I quit my job to work as a freelance illustrator. Bohemian life, here I come! I am broker than ever.

Even H&M is a luxury to me, as I hit rock bottom. It's the fashion juice cleanse. The only things I can't stop myself from buying are magazines. Dreams on paper . . .

I learn to shop in my closet, reinvent my old clothes, steal from my boyfriend, swap with my girlfriends. I also learn to mend, recut, and dye my clothes. I don't throw things away, I repurpose them, like I used to see my mom do. A man's shirt can be recut to make a super-cool skirt. Baggy pants can be worn super low with a belt to give a completely different look. A slipdress can be worn in the winter with a big sweater . . .

This shopping diet is actually a great way for me to find important elements of my style: men's clothes, coats, classics . . .

Having no money helps me understand that you don't need cash to be creative, fashionable, and cool. And, most important, I discover you don't need it to be happy.

I AM 33, I AM AN ILLUSTRATOR, AND I HAVE A BLOG!!!

Fashion blogs were born in France just as the fashion mass market exploded.

Zara, Topshop, H&M, and it's also the beginning of high–low designer collaborations (remember the war for a jacket by Karl Lagerfeld for H&M?). We are entering the years of over-shopping.

I am starting to make a living on my illustrations, and after the fashion juice cleanse, it's a total relapse: Instead of staying calm and buying just a few good pieces, I ruin myself with "good fashion deals" and lose my mind at stupid private sales.

I move to Paris and encounter the myth of the stylish Parisian firsthand, which is as depressingly real as can be. The cool girl I was in Marseille just doesn't measure up to the impossibly, effortlessly chic Parisian. On top of all that, I feel like I have to live up to the expectations of being a fashion blogger. I try to adjust, but it's the worst time of my life in terms of style.

I am not dressing for a guy, for my best friend, to look like my idol, to be special, or even for me: I'm dressing to try to be fashionable.

I buy the cheap version of whatever's on the runway, with no sense of myself. I wear things that don't flatter me, just because they're on trend.

Do you remember those baby-doll dresses that were all the rage when Phoebe Philo was at Chloé? Can you imagine me in a cheap version of a Chloé baby-doll dress? No? Me neither.

But I buy and wear them. If you find a photo of me wearing one, please throw it away. Really, these are the dark ages of my style. And the worst part is, I know it isn't working, but I have no idea what to do about it.

I learn that I'm not immune to the trends and that being a fashion victim is essentially being a victim. Yep. That's all I learn, but the lesson is totally worth it.

And at least it makes funny stories for the blog.

I'M 36, MY BLOG IS FAMOUS, AND I'M A FASHION-INDUSTRY INSIDER!

It's starting to sink in.

I'm understanding who I am, what I want, and what I don't want. I learn to say no. No to passing trends, no to cheap copies, no to things that don't flatter me.

I find my fundamentals: mixing menswear with feminine elements like skirts and high heels. I make my first fashion investments. An Hermès Kelly. A Burberry trench coat. A pair of Manolo heels.

I find my colors. I had known them forever— I was attracted to them naturally—but now they make my wardrobe. Whites, beiges, grays—and touches of red, blue, and green.

I still have moments where I panic and try to morph into sexy-cool Jenna Lyons or sexy-chic Carine Roitfeld, but moments like these usually don't last for long.

I still have a lot to learn. Evening dressing, for example, is still a challenge. And sometimes I freak out when the runway shows come around, because I feel like I have to dress the part. But I've come to realize that no matter what I do, I can't help but be me.

I'M 39, AND I HAVE REACHED FASHION MASTERY!!!

Just kidding.

I know what fits me and what makes me look good. I find myself buying the same thing over and over, but I don't mind—these are my classics, they always work, they always make me happy. You're going to learn everything about these essentials in the following pages.

I still make mistakes, but I've learned to ride the fashion-disaster dragon like a pro: I try new combos, new lengths, and new colors on days when it's safe to experiment—and on important days I stick with what works.

I know now that fashion can really empower and make anyone feel beautiful—and that missteps are not the end of the world. They're okay! They're fun! Nobody cares!

Style is a fascinating way to tune in to who we are, understand who we are not, be creative, and express our inner selves. ✗

NET-A-PORTER.COM

1. I love this photo, shot by Derek Henderson for *Vogue* Australia - a very fashionable version of me. 2. A day at work in New York City. 3. Front row at Chanel, trying to keep my cool. 4. Downtime, checking e-mails between shows.
5. A shot by Patrick Demarchelier for a Net-à-Porter international campaign, seen here in *V* magazine. 6. At Fashion Week, a more sophisticated version of me.
7. At the shows, in heels you can only wear to the shows.

LESSON LEARNED

The Scarf

*The setting is Paris, in the days when I was seeking the answers
to all of life's questions at crowded sample sales.*
In other words, I'm drowning in a sea of Rykiel pants that retrace
the past twenty years of fashion, from the proudest moments
to the most obscure. The only thing missing is the present—
this winter's collection—which I dream about night and day.

I'm lugging around a bag full of at least three pairs of 6ers,[1] a long cardigan—striped, of course—and a whole bunch of happy happy Rykiel-eries that I'll hurry to slip on as soon as I get them paid for.

Right then I run into my friend, beautifully and freshly scarved. The painful sting of jealousy is quick to follow. Led only by greed, I swan-dive into a box of scarves and emerge proud as can be with a green, silky-soft floral scarf. Around my shoulders it goes, and she has nothing to say but "wow".[2]

It feels so right. I need this scarf. How much is it? Not that I really care. "It will be mine," and "I do have a 401K," and other end-of-the-world thoughts run through my head. I find the nearest saleswoman and grab her by the collar, threatening her with the power of my 6ers if she doesn't give me the intel.

HER: Surprised look.

ME: Haggard look.

HER: Knowing, sardonic look.

HER: "But, madame, this isn't a scarf! It's the fabric we use to line the bottom of the bins!"

ME: Feeling like Jessica Stam falling down on the catwalk.

A few steps behind me, my friend can barely hold it together she's laughing so hard.

And what do you imagine I did?

I found the manager and told her she needed to give me the bottom-of-the-bin fabric. She says no. I say yes. She says no way. I say, "I'll pay!" She says, "We don't even give these to employees." I say, "Name your price." She says, "Okay, fine, wait here."

She comes back with a little box and says, "On the house."

I always say that in life there are those who carry a loaded gun and those who dig.[3]

Me, I dig. I persevere. I push through. And, sometimes, I triumph. ✕

1 Six inches of heel. My friend says it's a little drag queen. "Garance, put those down before you get hurt!"
2 This is the kind of vocabulary that comes out during the big sales in Paris, by virtue of the low prices around you: "wow," "ugh," "no way," "too expensive," "I'd break it," and, of course, "Wow, seriously crazy-good deal, you bitch."
3 Don't tell me you haven't seen *The Good, the Bad and the Ugly.*

How to find your Style

Knowing your style goes a long way.

It gives you the power to communicate without saying a word; it turns you into a discerning shopper, the editor in chief of your own wardrobe.

After years of very serious research, fashion missteps, and wrong purchases, I have discovered that personal style and boundless fashion bliss lie at the intersection of four cardinals.

1. WHAT YOU KNOW ABOUT YOURSELF.

Take heels. As much as I love them, I know that I have to save them for special occasions, evenings out, and business meetings.

My daily routine varies. I take pictures, I write bundled up on my couch, but I also walk all over town for meetings. My days sometimes end with a cocktail, sometimes at a concert, with no time to change in between.

To be fully present in the things I do, I know what I want: I want to look good, but I also want to be able to forget about my clothes.

That's why I try to have a wardrobe that works whether I'm in heels or flats. Then I swap depending on my activities. I adjust and adapt not only to suit my tastes but also to suit my lifestyle.

Knowing yourself is knowing the distance between your dream self and your real self.

Jessica de Ruiter at home in L.A.
Perfect relaxed elegance.

2. WHAT YOU KNOW ABOUT YOUR BODY.

Any body type can look beautiful, under the right conditions, but let's be honest: It's just easier to wear what you see on the runway if you're skinny and relatively flat-chested with narrow hips. It's boring, annoying, wrong, and sucks.

You know why it sucks?

Because it's not your body's fault; it's the designer's fault. Most clothes are cut to look good on models, and for any other body type, it will be a struggle to make them look great.

When I'm in a bad mood, I curse about it. When I'm in a good mood, I see it as an opportunity to narrow my choices and edit. And less (choices) is more (style).

I have long legs (yaaay!) but that makes for a rather short torso (boooo!), and I do have boobs (yaaay? I've never been so sure if it's a blessing or a curse).

These are three of the reasons why you will never see me wearing high-waisted pants (I look like the pants have taken over my whole body and my boobs are floating atop my belt. CUTE).

Other things, on the contrary, look really good on me. Skirts. Tuxedo jackets. Deep V-necks. The list is long enough to be part of what makes my style.

This is a great process to go through. Try, try, try, and cross things off the list. In other words, edit. That's how great style is revealed.

3. WHAT YOU WANT TO SAY.

Our clothes carry the message we want to convey to others, and it changes, depending on what we're going through in our lives.

Today I work in fashion, so I want to communicate to others that I'm poised and in control and that I mean business, which may or may not be true, but anyway.

When I was twenty I was in a rock band. I wanted to be different, a rebel. When I was thirty, I wanted to say I was an artist. I might not have done this consciously at the time, but now I do.

My wardrobe is made of richer, solid colors and blues, blacks, and a lot of whites that are of course my personal taste but also express harmony, function, and freedom.

Maybe tomorrow I will want to say I'm sexy or adventurous, and then maybe I'll add a whole new layer to my wardrobe. Maybe I'll get rid of other parts that don't feel like me anymore.

Knowing what you want to say makes clothes your best friends.

This page: Anna Grey, easy and sensual.
Opposite page: Marina Larroudé in Paris.
The ultimate blend of femininity and ease.

4. WHO YOU WANT TO BE.

This is the dimension of dreams. This is where you add that extra touch to your style that makes it an expression of your deeper self.

What are your dreams? The ones you might achieve and the ones that will always stay dreams? Those unattainable dreams are to be cherished as well; they say so much about who we are.

Are you reaching for a new career? Looking for love? Go on and dress for it.

Borrow from your dreams. Of being a movie star. A great lover. A great mother. A respected teacher. A free spirit. An astrologer. An artist. A painter, a sculptor.

Whatever they are, these dreams are ours and they make us.

They guide us in our style—and in our lives. ✕

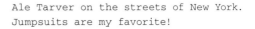

Ale Tarver on the streets of New York.
Jumpsuits are my favorite!

LESSON LEARNED

The Heels

NYC, Sunday, December 20, 2009, 3:00 p.m.

I'm ready to fly back to Paris, but huge snowstorms have me stuck in the Big Apple. Life can be *so* rough sometimes.

Blissed out at the idea of an unscheduled day, I decide to do what I love most in NYC—buy books and cupcakes. And then I'll go back to my hotel, make myself a cup of tea, and scarf down all three simultaneously.

I gear up for the tundra outside. Parka, pants, heavy socks, scarves, hat, big hood. When I can't see anything or move, that means that I'm ready.

And then . . . then.

I get all my shoes out . . . and I realize that NOTHING I have will help me brave the snow. Most of my shoes are heels (at the time, I hadn't yet found my style), and I love my few delicate pairs of flats too much to go walking out in the slush and salt (salt is terrible for shoes, TERRIBLE).

But I'm not gonna let a little snow stop me. I get out my platform-heeled boots, the ones with a thick crepe sole that'll keep me far above the slush—almost like mini-skis, if you look on the bright side, and, voilà, off I go down Bleecker Street and into the blizzard.

I walk like Master Yoda in *The Empire Strikes Back,* when he sends Luke into the cave. Mountains of slowly decomposing snow followed by pools of mud deeper than Kate Upton's neckline don't scare me. As long as I take it slow, I'll make it through. Yeah, bring it on, winter.

Except, after about three steps, I'm quite literally stuck.

I stand there pretending to check my phone. All around me, New Yorkers have gotten out their rubber boots. Stylish and practical, they make huge graceful bounds in the snow.

I'm jealous, but that won't hold me back. I'll make a little pit stop at Marc by Marc Jacobs, just next to Magnolia Bakery, where I'm sure to find some rubber boots for ten dollars.

A half hour later, I am still struggling to make it around the block. My hopes are flagging a little. There's a Starbucks up ahead, and I could always just get a muffin there and then get back inside and finally finish *Journey to the End of Night* instead of buying myself some gratuitous chick lit.

No. Not good enough. I've got to keep going. Prove it to the world (= to myself) that my love of heels won't get in the way of my life as a liberated woman.

I make a desperate plea (Give me any excuse not to finish that Céline—the author, not the brand, shallow people!) and attempt a jump over a giant puddle . . . and suddenly my Chloé mini-skis are in motion, starting the fatal cascade: my vanity and me, hopelessly linked, heading face-first into a pile of snow.

Mortified, I make my retreat.

Adieu, cupcakes, Marc by Marc, and piles of chick lit.

Sometimes you have to forget fashion and put your rubber boots on. ✗

The French woman says no

"The French woman does not exist!
She is a myth!
Why waste your time on books about her secrets?
She's as much a mess as you are!"

This is the answer I give (with a heavy French accent) when I am asked about the secret of French style. But:

1. This is fake modesty, which is very French—I am actually pretty flattered.

2. If everybody talks about something, it means that it exists, right?

Ah, this myth of French chic—I've lived with it my whole life. And I certainly don't mind being associated with the long line of Catherines and Jeannes and Emmanuelles that it brings to mind.

So let's get to the bottom of it.

It starts with an attitude.

Jeanne Damas, the quintessential Parisienne.

ELEGANCE IS REFUSAL.

The French woman is nonchalant and will apply herself to carrying that stance in every aspect of her life. In France, we're not supposed to stand out too much. Wanting to show off is suspect. It doesn't mean matters of style and beauty are overlooked, but they are very carefully cultivated to look effortless and to not overshadow your neighbor.

That's why you won't see so many colors, crazy hairstyles, or exposed body parts on the streets of Paris. Fashion is a quiet, personal matter. You only get a few short years when it's okay to dye your hair pink (or shave it).

This page: Ana Kraš wearing one of my favorite staples, a striped top. Opposite: High waists don't really work on me, so I love them even more on others!

SHE SAYS NO
TO WHAT DOESN'T
FLATTER HER.

The secret is to own your imperfections. No hiding them or trying to change them—you learn to make something interesting out of them. And clothes are there to help, not to be instruments of torture. They're at our service.

Our mothers teach us very early on to say no to any type of clothing that doesn't fit or flatter us.

"My love, pants just don't look good on you; you should only wear skirts!"

Sounds pretty rough, no? But style education is serious business. And when she has found what works for her, the French woman sticks to it.

Emmanuelle Alt and her skinny jeans that make her legs look longer than the Eiffel Tower. Carine Roitfeld and her midi skirt, so strong and sexy. Caroline de Maigret and her bangs and forever-messy hair.

We find what works, and and we're not afraid to say no to everything else.

SHE SAYS NO TO TRENDS.

Trends are fun to read about in a magazine on a Sunday morning, and shopping is a perfect time to catch up with friends, but that's about where it ends.

The French woman will only buy a trendy item if she is sure she can make it work in her wardrobe, but being too on trend is suspect, means you're a fashion victim, and—horror!— that you want to stand out.

SHE SAYS NO TO SWEATPANTS.

You'll rarely see a French woman in her gym clothes, unless she is actually at the gym, which is rare because she also likes to say no to going to the gym, but that's another subject for another day. It's just not done. And even though these rules are getting lost as we get more and more influenced by, hmm, American TV, French people still really make a distinction between the interior life (at home) and exterior life (outside, dressed up).

I like going outside in my gym clothes, by the way. It is very un-French of me.

This page: Jessica Joffe,
a beautiful way to wear black.
Opposite: Lisa Jones, making
head-to-toe denim her own.

SHE SAYS YES, FOREVER, TO HER CLASSICS.

Things that last are cherished. Classics are revered, passed from generation to generation. It can be your chic grandmother's Kelly or your mom's gold necklace.

Important moments in the life of a French woman include buying her first watch, her first perfume, her first bag—these are important because there is a chance she might wear them every day and forever.

If she likes a certain kind of T-shirt, she won't hesitate to buy three. This will become her signature. If she likes a certain type of red lipstick, she will go ahead and stock up (the worst moments of a French woman's fashion life being when her favorite things get discontinued. I've seen a friend buy forty-five bottles of perfume, trying to do the math to see if it would last for the rest of her life).

Knowing her style means knowing that what she loves today, she'll love forever. Knowing her style also means that once she has it down, she can stop thinking about fashion. Because fashion fades.

But style . . . It's a big yes, forever. ✕

Melissa Bon knows how to elevate her classics, in one of my favorite essentials, the leopard coat.

LESSON LEARNED

The Clutch

I arrive at the café, ready for a night out and rather thrilled at the prospect of spending the evening with one of my most Parisian friends.

The sort who knows the city like the back of her hand, kisses everyone on two cheeks when she gets to the Flore, and drives around in her Smart car at an insane speed, not to start any rumors about Parisian behavior.

She is so cool, you see. So much Frencher than I am.

There she is, sitting pretty, with her messy hair and her red lips and her cigarette and her what-do-I-care look. A page straight out of Paris *Vogue,* right in front of me.

Then my eyes lock on her Hermès clutch.

"Peeeeerfection!!!" I say as I grab it from her. (How American of me.)

"Oh, it's just an old thing my mom gave me." (How Parisian of her.)

"Oh, come on, now, that is pretty much a treasure. I've never seen one like it—and that color! It's, like, the perfect shade of butter! And I love butter! Aaaaaahh loooove jealooooouuusyyy faaaashion hysteriiaaaaa." (How American of me.)

"Garance, beware, you sound like a New Yorker!" she says with a wink. (How Parisian of her.) "This is just a bag; who cares!" And takes a drag of her cigarette.

Two of our other friends arrive at that moment, and it's time to go.

We end up at a party and one hour and three glasses of champagne later, I'm dancing on tables. My friend is also really enjoying herself but in a much more I'm-too-cool-to-care

type of way, meaning she is neither dancing on the tables nor shouting out the lyrics along with strangers. Instead she is talking secretively with someone while moving her shoulder to the music—the obvious sign that she is having a lot of fun. And the butter clutch is lying loosely by her side, as if she has forgotten its existence.

Suddenly, a girl rounds the corner with a big glass of unidentified dark liquid and trips on something. The drink comes splashing down on my friend . . . and her beautiful Hermès clutch.

She turns white, looks at me, grabs the bag, her jacket, and flees.

We follow and find her sitting on the side-walk, looking at her clutch, heartbroken.

We try to comfort her but, really, she is inconsolable.

Needless to say, we don't go back to the party.

I guess this was the night my friend reached the limits of her French coolness.

We all still mourn the bag, and sometimes we find ourselves back at the café, remembering how beautiful the butter clutch was.

And no one has ever said: "Oh, come on, now, it's just a bag!!!"

I don't think it would be met with a French shrug.

Even the most effortless French girl has her limits. ✗

This is one
of my favorite
coats and it
is from Zara.
I've had it for
years!

MIX HIGH AND LOW

I know I talk about it too much, but I love to shop at Zara.

I'm a bit of an expert, and I can say this with confidence because I have been refining my skills for many years.

Zara has evolved with me. At first I could barely afford it, and today I mix it with designer pieces. My Zara mastery is so impressive that random strangers (okay, my friends) throw themselves at my feet (okay, they text me) for my advice.

Stop throwing yourselves at me, people! It's so easy! Here are my secrets.

1. GO OFTEN.

Zara gets new shipments in all the time, and good things don't stay on the racks for long.

The store I go to gets shipments in on Thursdays. So the best thing to do is stop by on my way home to see if a Zara miracle happened overnight. Online is even better: The new stuff is just a click away. The downside is that you can't try it on and touch the fabric.

2. IDENTIFY THE COLLECTIONS.

Going often is actually super easy because, once you get the hang of it, you'll be in and out in five minutes, max. For example, I rarely venture into the back of the store.

I look around right at the entrance: That's where the most attractive clothes are.

If I don't see anything, I flip a 180 and out I go.

AAAAAAOOOOOHHHHH YEAHHHH! (ZARAGASM)

3. ZERO IN ON THE BEST PIECE.

Here's the heart of our mini-guide.
(Picture me in front of a blackboard with my pointer stick in the air, please.)

The piece.

The piece is rare. It feels almost separate from the rest of the shelf.

It stands alone in its beauty, waiting for you to spot it and take it home.

Let's say it's a coat—though it can also be a bag, a shirt, or a beautiful pair of pants.

Bring your hand to the fabric and touch it. It should feel refined. Check the tag to see what it's made of. The cut and details are almost perfect.

Uh-oh ... Wait ... Wait ... Oh, oh, ooooooh!

Aaaaaaooooohhhhh yeahhhh! (Zaragasm.)

The piece you are standing in front of was created for exactly this reason—so that when people compliment you, they'll say, "No way you got that at Zara!!!"

The piece is not what will make the store money—it's there for prestige, to stand out, as living proof that they make great things.

Sometimes the price of the piece is a little higher than usual. But I'm telling you, it won't be there in three hours. Buy it and don't look back.

4. ATTENTION!!!

Avoid getting overly excited about the piece that looks a little too "inspired by." I know, it's tempting, but if it looks too much like Marant, Céline, or Valentino, step away.

If nothing more, out of respect for the designers.

But also because wearing a copy doesn't send the best message. Not to ourselves or to others. As with everything—staying chic is knowing when to resist temptation. ✕

Lais Ribeiro, in a
story I shot for *Vogue*
Brazil, styled by Viviana
Volpicella. I love the
subtle eccentricity of
her look.

It's o.k.
to break the rules

So there you are, with all of your perfectly edited, perfectly tailored, perfectly timeless pieces.

Don't you feel so at peace, like you've just done an hour and a half of yoga and had a green juice?

You know what happens to me after an hour and a half of yoga and a green juice?

I want to go have a cocktail! I want to call my friends!!! I want to go crazy!

The same goes for your wardrobe.

There are moments when you need to let loose. Buy a totally incongruous fashion item that nobody other than you and the designer understands.

Shoes you can't walk in. Who said you have to walk in shoes?

A coat that will scream "Autumn-winteeeeeeer 200000015555!!!" to anybody who listens. A pair of furry Céline Birkenstocks. A vintage unidentified . . . is that a onesie?

Should you give in to your impulses? There are two ways to answer that.

1. DO THE FASHION EQUATION, AKA CALCULATE YOUR COST PER WEAR.

Take that pink fake-fur coat you want to buy. How many times are you going to wear it?

Divide the price by that number and you have your Cost Per Wear. Be honest. And remember that:

× Standout items can't be worn too often unless you want to become "the girl with the crazy pink fake-fur coat."

× Runway items will feel out of date after three to six months.

× Salespeople are paid to say, "This is very wearable."

2. USE ANY EXCUSE THAT'S AT YOUR DISPOSAL TO CAVE AND PURCHASE THE CRAZY ITEM.

Okay, so you've decided to be bold. But beware of these pitfalls:

× You're virtually loaded! You just got a call that you might get a new, very important (and well-paid) commission.

This is almost always a mistake, but every freelancer in the world does it, so I am not going to throw stones. I may or may not have bought a Balenciaga coat two minutes before receiving a phone call telling me that the job was actually canceled.

My advice: Maybe wait till the job is confirmed?

× You're going on a first date.

Wrrrrong!!! Most people don't like to be blinded by a crazy fashion item—you are the one who needs to shine. Unless your date is with Anna Dello Russo. But then, you wouldn't want to steal her thunder, would you?

× Your idol, Lady Gaga, would totally wear it.

We don't get to choose who we idolize. Go for it.

× You don't have any ten-inch heels in your wardrobe.

True. But just because they exist doesn't mean you have to own a pair. Unless you're a mob wife.

× It's soooo cheap.

Yes, sometimes the craziest things are also the cheapest. Warehouse-sale triple markdown? Maybe there's a reason? You don't see one? Just wait. But either way, not too risky.

We all need to go crazy once in a while. If it's not too often, it can even breathe new life into an otherwise too perfectly balanced wardrobe. Perfect is boring. ✗

MOST PEOPLE
DON'T LIKE
TO BE BLINDED BY
A CRAZY FASHION
ITEM — YOU ARE
THE ONE WHO
NEEDS TO SHINE.

What is a tuxedo?

I consulted with four fashion experts, and none of
them could give me an exact answer.
We all agreed on the fact that a tuxedo is a jacket-and-
pants ensemble and that you can add a vest to it.

We also agreed on its name. It's called Yves after its
creator, Mr. Saint Laurent, who apparently liberated
women by giving them the option of dressing like a man.

All of us had a satin collar in mind.
Some of us said the pants had to be pleated, but that's
where opinions started to diverge:

× "You have to wear it with a tie!"

× "The pants have to have a satin stripe down the side!"

× "Tuxedos have to be black."

That last comment sent the conversation
teetering into a high-pitched screaming match,
so let's get to the bottom of it.

DOES THE TUXEDO HAVE TO BE BLACK?

"No! It can be any color. It can be red, it can be off-white, it can be white. Just ask Bianca Jagger!" (Google "Bianca and Mick Jagger wedding.")

SHOULD YOU WEAR IT WITH NOTHING UNDERNEATH?

That's how Betty Catroux did it.

I'm not that daring, personally, but I give my full respect to women who are.

HOW DO YOU FEEL WHEN YOU GO OUT IN A TUX?

This is something every woman should experience.

Once you've slipped into a tuxedo, something happens.

First of all, you can move around freely. The pants, oh, the pants! You can hop onto a motorcycle with perfect ease if you feel like it. And the jacket! The jacket frames and liberates your body. Everything looks perfect from every angle.

Then you put on extra-high heels.

And that's how you make your entrance, looking like the girl who's going to have the most fun at the party. Because you (may have) just arrived on a motorcycle. And also because all the other women are wearing dresses, so you stand out while still fitting in perfectly.

And at that moment, marvel of marvels, you realize that your tuxedo is not only getting you looks from the guys but also compliments from the women.

WHAT TO DO IF ANOTHER WOMAN IS WEARING A TUXEDO AT THE PARTY.

Remember that when you wear a tuxedo, you are armed with a heroic, self-deprecating sense of humor. I'd say go kiss the other woman square on the mouth. Do it for a long time and in front of photographers.

It's a great thing to do and can even give a good kick to a dormant career. Ask Madonna.

HOW TO CHOOSE YOUR TUXEDO.

Choose freely. Of course, your first impulse, as a fashion-lover, will be to go to Saint Laurent or to try to find a vintage one, and you'd be right.

But I have to admit that I found mine somewhere else and it's fabulous.

It's Stella McCartney, and I found it on a day I wasn't even looking for one. Everything was there. The double-breasted jacket, extremely well cut, trimmed in satin. The pants were pleated and cuffed, and there was something about them that immediately won me over: They were designed to be worn slightly short. And, of course, the white blouse *and* black shoes were there too. I took it all.

YOU'LL BE READY IN SEVEN MINUTES FLAT, SAID LOULOU DE LA FALAISE.

WHAT ABOUT THE POCKET SQUARE? SHOULD YOU WEAR ONE?

Of course! That's what will make you a real man.

And by that I mean someone who really knows the male dress code and isn't afraid to have fun with it. Don't try to fold it every which way—you aren't on the cover of *Monsieur* magazine. A pretty, artistic blur of silk is enough.

SHOULD YOU ACCESSORIZE TO DEATH?

Adding some bling is a choice. Either Catherine Deneuve or Rihanna.

HOW LONG DOES IT TAKE TO PUT ON A TUXEDO? IS IT COMPLICATED?

You'll be ready in seven minutes flat, said Loulou de la Falaise.

CLUTCH OR HANDS IN YOUR POCKETS?

Having your hands in your pockets is not just a matter of posture; it's the entire history of the tuxedo, because having somewhere to put your hands gives you unbelievable confidence.

The way you move changes completely—your balance changes, your energy is different.

The spark that you gain could be lost with a clutch.

It happens to me all the time—I have this pretty little thing in my hand that's just for decoration, since I have absolutely no room to put anything in it.

If I take a glass of champagne, both my hands are full and I can't shake anyone's hand, not even if it's Marc Jacobs, who's just come over to say hi and now thinks I'm very rude.

CAN A FRENCH GIRL SAY, "TONIGHT I'LL PUT MY SMOKING ON!" TO AN AMERICAN MAN?

Oh la la, get ready for a look of horror. In America, *le smoking* is called a tuxedo. The guy is already terrorized (and titillated!) by the fact that you're French, that you don't even hide your cigarettes, that you go topless on the beach and gobble up escargot in garlic butter at all hours of the day and night.

Reassure him, French girls. Say: "Tonight I'll put my tuxedo on, honey."

CAN YOU WEAR *LE SMOKING* IN A *NONSMOKING* RESTAURANT?

Hahaha.

CAN YOU WEAR A TUXEDO TO A BLACK-TIE PARTY?

Now that the term "black tie" has been reduced to nothing by party organizers with delusions of grandeur, it's nearly impossible to get a clear idea of the dress code. Especially in fun, messy, haughty Paris, where we love wearing jeans to a fancy party.

So, if you want to look too cool for the party, while still being polite to your hosts, the tux is your best friend.

CAN YOU WEAR A TUXEDO TO A BUSINESS MEETING?

Poor girl. Do you really want to destroy the power of the tuxedo? I didn't think so.

Save it for the night.

CAN YOU WEAR A TUXEDO MORE THAN ONCE?

The tuxedo is a secret agent. It makes you beautiful without being obvious about it. It's the opposite of a sublime evening gown that everyone remembers even better than they remember you. You know, the kind you can only wear once, no matter how much you love it, because everyone will notice.

Not the case with the tuxedo. With our dear tuxedo, you can:

Wear it again without anyone noticing.

Slip it into your bag in case of an unexpected party.

Mix it up. Wear the top without the bottoms, and vice versa.

Change what you wear underneath, which changes the whole feel of your tux.

Put it on when nothing seems to be going well and you've gained five pounds.

The problem: You end up wearing it all the time.

And here, my friends, is the danger.

The tux is a trap. It works its magic on you and leaves you with no common sense. Caught in its web, you forget what other clothing has to offer. If you aren't careful, you'll end up wearing nothing else. You never wear dresses anymore. You forget what it's like to let a little skin show. You become predictable.

You become the girl in the black tuxedo.

Beware. ✕

Jana Wirth in a perfectly fitted tuxedo.

My style essentials

A perfectly edited wardrobe can set you free. You will need less, and buy better. These are my style essentials, my forever classics on which I build anew every season. They make working, partying and traveling easier. They define my style, and some of them may come to define yours, too.

THE PENCIL SKIRT

This is the perfect piece that you can dress up (with heels and a blouse) or dress down (with a pair of sneakers). It's flattering, it says you're a real woman who owns her shit, and it's perfect at night or for an important meeting. I love this one in lace by Dolce & Gabbana.

THE PUMPS

A perfect, pointy pump makes everything better — and I'm not just talking about outfits! These off-white suede Manolo Blahniks are my go-to pair (sexy AND comfortable), but my goal is to have them in every shade one day. (Opposite page)

THE WHITE JEANS

These are my personal
favorite, for summer and
winter. I like them a
little bit cropped to show
some ankle. Seen here on
Lolita Jacobs.

THE BOOTS

Chelsea boots are a girl's
best friend, especially
in winter. They work
with jeans and skirts,
and they're warm and
comfortable. My favorites
are Church's.

THE BAG

I love love love the Lulu
by Saint Laurent Paris.
It's perfectly luxurious and
discreet at the same time.
The essence of chic!

THE BIKER JACKET

This is an investment
you'll never regret
because it becomes
your best friend.
Here, Laura Vidrequin
in her Céline jacket.

THE SNEAKERS

We all need a pair and
there are so many great
options from Converse,
Adidas, Vans. But these
are my personal favorites,
by Common Projects.

THE COAT

Lara Melchior in a belted
wrap coat — an essential
that goes with everything,
night and day. I love it in
a dark navy.

THE VINTAGE T-SHIRT

This piece adds the rock 'n' roll (and a touch of irony) that a wardrobe needs, and Kate Foley pulls it off perfectly. Easy to find (with a little hunting) in thrift stores and it only gets better with age (even those holes are all good!).

THE JEAN JACKET

Seen here on Michele Ouellet, the classic jean jacket is a great layering piece. It works for any season and gets more beautiful every year.

THE PANTIES

Simple, light, and white.
Enough said! Commando
makes the perfect pair,
and Jessica Vasconcelos
wears them pretty well.

THE BALLERINE

No need to explain why we all need a
pair (or five) of ballerines, even if
just to keep in our bags for relief
after a long day in heels. Porselli is
my favorite brand because they work
perfectly with the shape of my foot.

THE MEN'S SHIRT

Always in my suitcase, because it works from night to day to beach to city. Perfectly accessorized here by Viviana Volpicella.

THE WHITE T-SHIRT

So simple and easy, I wear
one almost every day during
summer. It's like a blank
canvas you can create
any outfit around. My
favorite is classic Fruit
of the Loom, seen here on
Alessandra Codhina.

THE V-NECK SWEATER

Cashmere with a deep V is the way to go (I love Equipment's). Perfectly sensual, and warm, as seen here on Athina Elaiya.

THE SANDALS

It's tough to choose my
favorites because I have
a weakness for sandals,
but I've owned a pair
of Rondinis for years
and they never go out of
style. And their barely-
there quality is so
beautiful and sexy.

THE HAT

Shot on Jessica Vasconcelos,
the straw hat doubles as a
style and a beauty essential.
We need to protect our faces
from the sun in summer and
nothing is cooler and more
elegant than a panama.

THE CLUTCH

A classic black clutch is the
perfect finish to evening wear,
but it also works beautifully with
jeans, so it's all love! It's the one
object where I don't mind a little
logo, especially one as sophisticated
as the YSL Cassandre.

THE GLASSES

The Wayfarer, the Aviator,
the Clubmaster — it's impossible to
choose between the Ray-Ban classics.
They are all forever cool and they
work on just about every face shape.
You can buy all three for the price
of a single designer pair.

THE MINI SKIRT

I spend my summers
in skirts. With flats,
they are easy and feminine.
With heels, they are sexy.
And I really don't mind
sexy, once in a while.
Morgane Bedel wears it
perfectly.

THE BLAZER

Every season, every
occasion, everywhere.
A basic, beautifully cut
blazer goes with absolutely
everything, never gets
old, and always adds a
sophisticated touch, as
seen on Camilla Engstrom.

THE MAILLOT

The Eres one piece is the perfect
investment, in black or white,
as seen here on Natasza Wasilewski.
A simple one piece makes you feel
beautiful, works for the beach or the
pool, and never goes out of style.

ON STYLE

ONE ON ONE WITH A WOMAN WHO INSPIRES ME

Emmanuelle Alt

GD: Your style is so recognizable. How would you define it?

EA: So many people think they need to dress according to fashion or a certain brand. But style is about harmony and having self-confidence. It's knowing yourself.

GD: What about dressing for your body type? Do you try to do that?

EA: I wear what I feel good in. One of the most important things for me is to feel at ease. There's nothing worse than spending an evening in a piece of clothing that makes you feel unlike yourself.

GD: You don't really wear evening gowns. And I'm similar — I don't like dresses either.

EA: For me, femininity is in no way tied to wearing a dress or a skirt. I think you can be incredibly feminine in pants.

GD: Everyone loves to ask me, "What is the secret of French style?" How would you answer that?

EA: For French women, there's not the same pressure. If someone tells me I have to go to a party and I have nothing in my closet, I'm going to improvise. I'll put on a black blazer, a white T-shirt, some mascara, some heels. And I'm ready to go. There's not that state of panic.

GD: What do you consider sexy?

EA: Sexy, I think, is a smile. It's a sense of humor. It's someone who is at ease, funny. That's sexy. Much sexier than a dress code.

GD: Have you ever seen yourself in a photo and thought, Oh, God, what was I thinking?

EA: Sure, but then . . . I've stopped looking at myself in photos.

LIFE OF THE PARTY

Parisians don't party like New Yorkers. And vice versa.
I have a theory about the difference, my friends.
It comes down to this:

THE PARISIAN NIGHT IS PRIVATE.
THE NEW YORK NIGHT IS PUBLIC.

I had to confront this cultural gap as I was about to move to New York City. One night, I was out at the Boom Boom Room and I told a friend about my plan to move to New York.

The next day, bam. It was up on a magazine's blog. Someone had overheard our conversation and had simply decided to go ahead and make it into a story. A few hours later, it had raced around the Web, and I only found out because I got a flurry of texts saying things like:

"Congrats on your move to NYC, Garance!"

"Amazing news!!! Can't wait to have you over for dinner!"

"How come I have to learn about that online?"

And that's how a private conversation that shouldn't have been of interest to anyone except my friends became a piece of news. That'll teach me to babble about my personal life at the Boom Boom Room.

But how was I to know? This sort of thing would never happen in Paris. Gossip blogs don't even exist in France. We don't have "Page Six" (the super-popular gossip page in the *New York Post* that everybody pretends not to read), and we have *vie privées,* private lives.

In Paris, the concept of *vie privée* really means something—basically, unless you're the president, private matters stay private. Which isn't to say that gossip doesn't circulate, but it stays pretty hush-hush and we keep it in smaller circles.

New York is different. New York is a planet unto itself. New York has its own celebrities, designers, entrepreneurs, sons of, wives of, all of which you wouldn't ever talk about in Paris.

New York has its own magazines, and any given party has its photographers. Parties are dissected like they're the event of the century: "Who was there? And with whom? What dress was she wearing? What shoes? What jewelry? Wait, what?! The same as last time? OH MY GOD, I can't believe it. Who's her publicist? Don't tell me she doesn't have one. Wait, what? She wasn't wearing her wedding band? Wait, zoom in. Let's take a closer look!"

New York created the socialite. It's a city where you go out to be seen and take part.

WHEN IT COMES TO FASHION, THE RESULT IS TWO VERY DISTINCT STYLES.

When the Parisian goes out, her goal is to be cool. The coolest.

It's that simple. She's not going to a party unless her friends are invited too, and she would rather die than be seen without her crew. You don't intermingle too much in Paris. You don't network, and if you do, you do so super discreetly: Networking means you need others, and needing others is terribly uncool.

Don't even try to do a seating arrangement at your dinner in Paris. People will completely ignore it and just sit with their friends.

Also, you'd better know that the Parisian will do everything she can to avoid being photographed, because wanting to have your picture taken is way too try-hard. She dresses in her eternal outfit of jeans and high heels with her hair down. Because, really, getting dressed up means you care. She's got better things to do.

Of course, in truth, she spends an hour on each smoky eye and five on her perfectly undone hair.

But what she's really into is having fun in small circles, pretending she isn't looking at the other little group over there in the corner. It's no surprise that the most popular clubs in Paris are small, darkly lit, smoky, and full of hidden nooks.

Our New Yorker, on the other hand, wants to be seen.

She gets her outfit ready a week ahead of time. She borrows a dress from a PR friend, who can't wait for the next morning to count the number of mentions her little protégée got her. She books a makeup artist and a hairdresser to give her the perfect blowout and makes sure that she gets to the party with all the right people—meaning important enough to make her look good but not so important that they outshine her.

If it gets too complicated, she goes alone.

She's on a mission to meet people and look good. Probably better to be alone in those pictures anyway.

That's not to say that everyone doesn't have a good time, from one side of the Atlantic to the other. In New York just as in Paris, people like to party and they do it well. And when the two sides meet, that's when it gets *really* fun.

But you have to know a few unwritten rules before heading out into the night.

Or else, in Paris, you'll show up in an evening gown just like it said to on the invitation (while everyone else is in jeans or miniskirts), and in New York, you'll get there in a tracksuit when it says "casual" (and everyone else is in cocktail dress, updos and all).

When in doubt, just get there late.

We all know that it's once the photographers are gone that the party really starts. ✕

WHEN IN DOUBT, JUST GET THERE LATE.

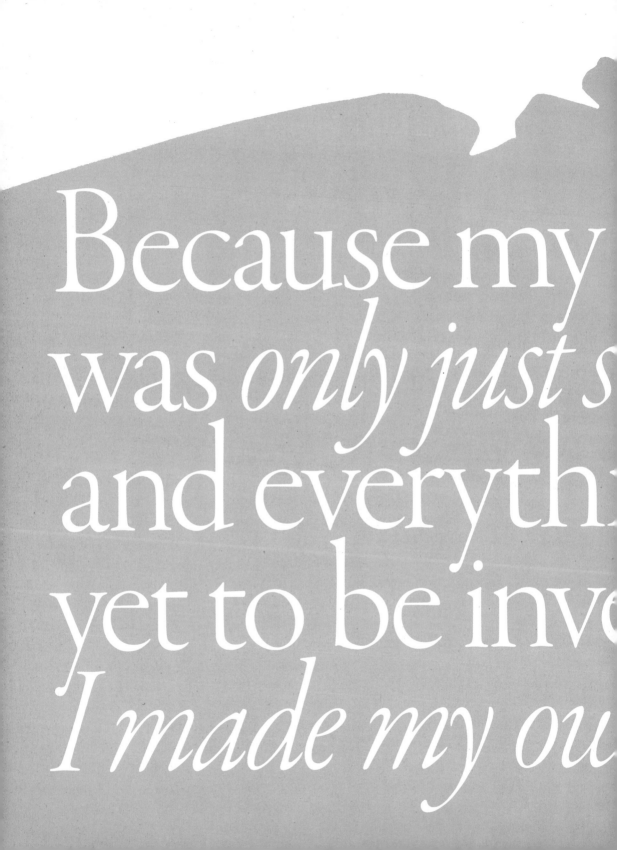

Because my
was *only just s*
and everythi
yet to be inve
I made my ou

world

arting,

ng was

nted,

rules.

THE 10 STEPS

This is how my story began. A computer, a name, and a dream.

START WHERE YOU ARE.

I was born in Ajaccio, a little seaside city on the west coast of the island of Corsica.

My parents were very beautiful, very much in love, and also completely broke. They were both the children of immigrants. My dad's parents were from Italy, and my mom's were from Algeria.

When they were both twenty, they got married and they had me.

My mom's family was Muslim, my dad's family was Catholic, so their wedding upset everyone and they were pretty much alone in the world. My dad had learned how to cook in his grandma's restaurant kitchen, and that's how one day he ended up becoming chef of the only restaurant in a tiny village called Girolata, lost in the middle of the Corsican wilderness.

There was no road or electricity there, but it was breathtaking. During summers, the jet set would sail in on their yachts and spend the night. And they would eat at my father's restaurant.

So there I was, a happy wild child watching princes and princesses and celebrities go up the tiny dirt path of our village, dressed beautifully, as they still did in the '70s. Think Brigitte Bardot, Gianni Agnelli, and Caroline of Monaco. The locals barely acknowledged their presence, which they loved.

I was dreamy and shy. I loved to read and draw. As I grew up, my parents asked me to pitch in and help at the restaurant. I did as I was told, but I absolutely hated it.

Eventually my parents opened their own restaurant in Girolata. We would spend summers there and winters in Ajaccio, where I went to school. My dad became a renowned chef and his restaurant a destination.

We started making money just as the bohemian '70s turned into the excessive '80s.

I grew into a very typical teenager—anxious, rebellious, annoying. But deep down I was still the same quiet and obedient kid I had always been. The day came when I had to start thinking about what I wanted to do with my life.

I told my parents that my dream was to follow an artistic path (I wanted to create animated movies, and I imagined myself spending my days drawing), but they wouldn't hear of it. Way too risky and impractical. Unfortunately, I had no other ideas. I knew nothing of the world. Corsica is an island where people are either farmers or shop owners, and if the books and magazines I was reading were showing me that there was more to the world elsewhere, I couldn't imagine how I would ever become part of it.

I wasn't used to opposing my parents, and there wasn't much I could say to convince them, so I gave in. And that's how I found myself picking my studies at random and following a friend to a big gray university in Marseille.

GET LOST AND FIND YOURSELF.

Losing yourself only takes a second, but finding your way back can take years.

That's what happened to me. I was twenty when I left Corsica for Marseille in the South of France. I found myself swallowed up by a giant university that I knew could spit me out at any second.

I was stressed and continually worried, but my world was changing.

I was meeting new friends. A lot of them were musicians and artists, and they made my time at university better. But still. Years went by and I was getting nowhere, treading water. I was studying communications, with disenchanted teachers who kept telling us how difficult it would be to find a job.

I started to believe that to live the artistic life I was dreaming of, I would have to give up comfort and security and scale back my expectations. So that's what I did. Drifting away from my studies, I told my parents to stop helping me financially. I couldn't stand being a burden.

As I was trying to figure out what to do with myself, I was living on boring jobs and learning to make it with little.

Which is pretty easy, actually, when you're part of a group of fun and happy and creative people. I spent those years constantly alternating between crazy anxiety (I was freaking out about my future) and wonderful moments. I had time for myself, a balcony with flowers I would water every day. I loved cooking for my friends, entertaining. I even had a cat.

Finally, I decided not to go back to university. I was twenty-six, I had spent way too long in college, and it wasn't getting me anywhere. My mom was so deeply disappointed (I had been such a talented kid!, she said) that she barely talked to me anymore.

There was pain in her eyes when she looked at me—it was terrible. I had always gone to her for guidance; I had wanted to make her proud. And now I was alone.

Deep down, I was disappointed in myself too, but I was mad at her for doubting me in the first place and not letting me study art—even though by now everything seemed to prove that she had been right.

But I didn't give up, and in a funny turn of events, fashion put my first mentor on my path. I had heard about an internship and sent my résumé to the Musée d'Art Contemporain in Marseille—the only place in the city that would make me feel anything close to the creative life I was craving.

I got an interview, and I was so excited that I bought a pair of terribly expensive boots to wear.

To give you an idea of how dire the situation was—after buying these boots, I was totally broke.

Maybe I needed to send a message to the universe.

FOLLOW THE SIGNS.

I interviewed with the museum's director, and the next day I got a phone call. But it wasn't the director. A man said: "I saw you yesterday at the museum—nice boots. Would you be interested in working with me at the museum's cinema? I'm looking for someone like you. Can I steal you from my colleague? She said it was okay."

And that's how I started working in cinema. I would be handling PR, and my new boss would teach me everything he knew about film. The internship was unpaid (I was still working another job) and I had no idea what I was doing—I had learned nothing practical from my studies. But I made it work.

I'd call my friends for help. "What's a 'press release'? What does it look like? Can you fax me one?"

(I know, fax.)

That's how I came to understand that I was able.

I was doing it. This was real, intellectual work. And I was good at it. Small things, but still. Bérard, my boss, was pleased with me. He was a great teacher. I had sensed that his phone call was one of those moments when life gives you a chance and I had been right to say yes. I was so happy.

Just when I began to think that I might try to make a career in cinema, I met an illustrator. I remember the moment perfectly. I was having a coffee with friends, and a charming blond girl sat down. A friend of a friend.

I asked her what she did and she said, "I'm an illustrator." I remember turning bright red, like I always do when I'm overcome with emotion.

I begged her to show me her studio and to talk to me about what she did. She agreed and we spent an afternoon together. At that point I knew next to nothing about what being an illustrator really meant—but something about it appealled to me. She answered all my questions that afternoon, and although it was not a lot to go on, it was everything I needed to decide I would give it a try.

It was finally time to act on that longing that had been deep down inside of me and that had come rushing back in a second.

I gave myself a year. If it didn't work, I decided, at least now I knew I could go back to a normal job.

One year to become an illustrator. I would quit all my little jobs. I needed to create a real sense of emergency.

Just imagine my mom's reaction.

RISK FAILURE.

I said goodbye to Bérard, showing him my first illustrations—which were a disaster (imagine his face). It was too late (and I was too broke) to go back to school to study illustration, so I decided I would teach myself. The plan was to put all my savings (I had none) toward trips to Paris, where I would show my work to art directors (I knew none).

I promised myself that I would show my work, no matter what.

The important thing was to get rid of doubt. Was I born to be an illustrator? Was it my calling? I couldn't go back to my previous life without being absolutely sure.

The risk of failure, of seeing my dreams crumble, somehow didn't scare me. I knew it was better than living with doubt. And anyway, I had already disappointed my family. I was already broke. I had nothing to lose, and I needed to know.

What a year that was. Trips back and forth between Marseille and Paris. So many closed doors. So many rainy days, lost in the Paris metro with my huge portfolio. So many nights on my friend Maelle's sofa. She was a saint: She never complained.

A year spent at my desk, learning to paint by studying other people's work and guessing at their techniques, doing a hundred bad drawings for one good one. The harsh feedback from art directors who were kind enough to open their doors to me. My first computer (which my dad paid for after a phone call that I hated to make: "Dad, I never ask, but this time I need you"), my first attempts on my graphics tablet, my first tries at building a website to create an online portfolio.

My first commission in a local magazine. And then in a national magazine.

I was an illustrator!!! Finally! Mooom, looook!!!

But I didn't have a second to sit back and enjoy my success—reality was knocking at the door, now more than ever. I learned that a half-page illustration in a magazine earned about three hundred dollars.

Crap!

An illustration took me about two weeks to make. I did the math.

I had accepted that an artist's life wouldn't be comfortable, but I suddenly realized that at this rate I would end up under a bridge, exactly as my mother had predicted.

USE WHAT YOU'VE GOT.

I had no choice. I would have to learn how to draw much faster. That's what I was determined to do.

If I could make an illustration in an hour, and if I could count on selling a ton of them (applause for my business plan, ladies and gentlemen!), it just might work.

I would have to train myself like crazy and totally change my illustration style. And this would have to happen three times faster than the first time around, because the clock was ticking. I decided to do everything on my drawing tablet, to speed up the process. And I knew I didn't have time to go back and forth to Paris anymore to bother random art directors. I had to find a way to get precise, honest feedback, fast.

I needed a new way of showing my work.

It was 2006, and at that time in France, people were just starting to talk about blogs. But there was no such thing as a blog that had known big success. And in those days blogs weren't very pretty or visual.

But at that moment I needed a way to put my work out there. Something quick and cheap, and a blog seemed like a good option. It was all that I had anyway. That and my imagination.

By building my online portfolio, I had already learned a bit of coding. I knew I could make it look nice and give it a rhythm.

I would publish an illustration every other day. I would time myself. An hour a post. No more.

Wait. But what if it failed?

Showcasing my work on the Internet was the most public thing I'd ever done. And, you know—in 2006 it wasn't cool at all to have a blog. It was definitely not something to brag about.

The reaction when you mentioned a blog was a bit like:

"I'm sorry, a what? A blog? What the hell does that mean?

All this is why I decided I would go with a *nom de plume.*

And because I'm not a huge fan of weird pseudonyms (yes, thinking about you, Lady Gaga), I decided to choose a name that felt like a real name. I gathered my three best friends, told them about my idea. I had thought about Doré already, because it's the name of one of the first illustrators I'd ever heard about. And one of my friends, Sarah, gave me the name Garance.

Garance Doré.

This is how my story began. A computer, a name, and a dream.

And an infinite dose of energy, bubbling up after years of failure and frustration.

FALL IN LOVE.

I fell in love with the medium.

I could never have imagined I would love blogging so much.

It was just about training myself to be a faster illustrator, in the beginning. I was only thinking I would get honest feedback that would help me improve. But something I'd never expected began to happen.

I actually loved sharing my work on the blog. I responded to everyone who wrote to me, tried to do better every day, thought about it every second. I was passionate.

I remember all of my "firsts" so vividly, like a love story.

The first time I posted an illustration. The doubt, but also the feeling of, What do I have to lose? Nobody can see me anyway.

The first time I posted a little text to go along with an illustration. My first comment.

The first blogger who linked to me, sending me a ton of new visitors.

The first time a post got eighteen comments. I called my boyfriend: "Ooooooh myyyy goddd, this is craaaaazyyy!!!"

And everything that followed. I loved, LOVED, what I was doing. It didn't bring me any money—nobody would have even thought about monetizing a blog at the time. But for the first time in my life, I adored my work. And I felt like I was not so bad at it.

People were encouraging me. I had fans! Unknown people from unknown places would visit the blog every day to tell me they loved my stories and my illustrations.

To this day, it's still the thing that brings me the most joy.

I talked a lot about fashion on the blog because I loved it. I had always been an avid reader of fashion magazines, and I'd always believed that through fashion one can express almost anything, from the most superficial to the most profound.

Obviously, my one-hour rule didn't last long. I even remember spending a whole vacation waking up before my friends just to have a few hours to myself to write for my blog.

In other words, I was crazy in love.

SEIZE THE MOMENT.

I didn't know it at the time, but I had created something completely new.

Without even thinking, I had caught a wave that was about to change everything.

There were blogs; there were illustrators. There were fashion lovers.

But I was the first fashion-loving illustrator with a blog. Magazines started to call, wanting to interview me. At first I didn't want to show my face—it was one of the reasons I had changed my name—but that didn't last long.

People started calling to offer me illustration commissions. Better jobs. Better pay. I had decided I would never mention that I was not living in Paris. I had come to realize during my visits that living in Marseille was not looked upon favorably by the fashion world.

That proved to be a smart decision, but it made my life pretty complicated.

My boyfriend didn't want to leave the South of France, but I could sense this was my moment. People were calling me for meetings, never imagining that I could be living anywhere other than Paris. So I decided to go, just to give it a chance. With my tiny budget, I would only be able to survive there for a couple of weeks.

But I was going to Paris!!! The city I'd never even dared to dream of.

It was a tough landing. Paris is a gray city. People don't have time for you. Apartments are small, even more so when you're broke. It was like being a student again. I was thirty-one and living on a convertible sofa.

But for the first time in my life, I was passionate about what I was doing. I was happy. I was working like crazy, but it was not work. It was pure fun.

I even started to make a little money.

My blog was a window into my work, so people called me for illustrations but also to write for them. Supreme surprise: I had never thought about my writing as something people were seriously interested in. I considered my readers my friends. I wrote the way I talked. It wasn't an effort; I didn't have to search for a style. I didn't care about being perfect; I just loved expressing what I felt, simple words and energy.

Moving to Paris was the craziest decision of my life, but it was also my moment of opportunity: Paris was the place where my life was waiting for me. I never went back to Marseille.

QUESTION YOUR BELIEFS.

For a long time I believed that I shouldn't ask for too much. That it was shameful to be ambitious.

And it wasn't even on my radar when I first got to Paris, but do you know what happens there twice a year? Fashion Week.

In 2007, Paris Fashion Week was not the super-publicized event it is today. There were no street-style darlings, no livestreams. Style.com was just starting. Oh, and there was that guy, the Sartorialist, who was taking photos of people on the street.

I decided to go and check it out with a friend. "Take your camera!" she said.

That's how two things happened at the same time:

> 1. I discovered I had a talent for photography.
>
> 2. I fell in love, again.

As I took my first steps in the Tuileries, the center of the Fashion Week universe at the time, a friend casually introduced me to Scott Schuman, the Sartorialist. Meeting him was not only the beginning of a friendship that ended in a love story.

To me, it was like meeting America.

It was simple. In the beginning, we spent our time fighting. We would run into each other between shows and chat. That's the way our friendship started. Our ways of

thinking were totally opposite, and we would inevitably clash over something.

He didn't understand anything about my ways.

Like the way I was talking about my blog, for example:

"It's only a hobby! It's not my work! I'm an illustrator!"

He said that I was thinking small. Or the way I talked about other bloggers:

"What would they think if I started taking myself seriously and tried to really make something out of the blog?"

He said I was letting the opinion of others keep me down. Or investing in a better camera:

"Why would I do that? My photos are just for fun! I'm not a photographer; I'm an illustrator."

He said I was putting myself in a box.

I would argue, but I always ended up listening. Deep down I wanted to believe in his anything-is-possible American point of view. I wanted to believe him when he said "If you know how to create emotion, you can create a business" (horrified shout on my end). He challenged me, made me question my own beliefs, and it was tough—but I could feel the world slowly opening up to me. I was opening my eyes.

MAKE YOUR OWN RULES.

I decided it was time to break the mold. My blog could be more than just illustrations. I started to take photography more seriously. I published my first photos on the blog.

Publishing photos had an impact I could have never imagined. The immediacy of the photos, the fact that you didn't need words to understand them, took the blog to a whole new level.

It became completely international.

Along with the photos came travel—the more popular the blog became, the more I was called to travel around the world to take photos. It was constant. I was not even really living in Paris; I was not really living anywhere.

That's when the blog exploded.

I started to get serious job offers. Shoot a big editorial for a fashion magazine. Meet the editor in chief. Write my own column. Sell ads on my blog at a moment when I didn't even know how or how much. Shoot an ad campaign for a brand, get shot for a magazine, attend a gala, sit in the front row of a fashion show. I had never done any of it before.

It sounds like a dream, but I had no one to guide me. I didn't know anything about the delicate, nuanced rules of the industry that was about to open its doors very wide to me. I may have made a few mistakes.

But had I known the do's and don't's of fashion, I would most certainly not be where I am today. I would have been too scared, too intimidated. I would have stopped dead in my tracks—so I guess my innocence and ignorance worked in my favor.

I had learned how to learn as well. To make something from nothing. To ask questions, to surround myself with good people and believe in my instincts.

And because my world was only just starting, and everything was yet to be invented, I made my own rules.

From there, things happened really fast. The blog became bigger. I was getting recognized on the street. People would call me and ask to be featured on the blog. I would be invited to be on TV shows, offered crazy jobs, book deals. I had to learn to say no. I moved to New York. I was featured in *The New York Times*. I received a CFDA Award, the highest recognition you can receive in fashion. It's like the Oscars. And this was the first ever CFDA Award to be given to a blogger. Times were changing.

YOU HAVE TO
CREATE YOUR OWN
DEFINITION OF
SUCCESS.

FOLLOW THE ENERGY.

That brings us to today.

I still remember that day in Paris when, exhausted by the amount of work I had to do, I hired an assistant to help me with my e-mail. That was the beginning of Garance Doré Studio.

All right—let's talk about the name. You know why I called it the Studio? Because when I started, I was living and working in my tiny Paris studio. "Studio" gave me a big, bold feeling, but it was pretty ironic. Each time I think about it, I crack up.

It's amazing to think back on it now that I have a real studio that's big and bright and with a view of the New York skyline.

And a real team that I love.

I remember one piece of advice that Scott gave me when I was feeling confused by the pressure of success and all of the questions that it raised.

What should I do with all of it?

Make as much money as possible?

Try to become "someone" in fashion?

Go on TV and become a celebrity?

Continue on without changing anything?

He told me: "You have to create your own definition of success."

For some, success might mean a career as a teacher, shaping young lives.

For others, it's being on the cover of *Vogue*.

It took me a very long time to arrive at my own definition. I gave it time and learned to follow my instincts, and it slowly became obvious.

To me, success means being part of a creative conversation and, above all, feeling free. It means being surrounded by a team you love and working in a beautiful, inspiring place.

And, to make these things happen, I learned to trust myself and follow the energy. The energy of places, of people. The energy I feel but also the energy I put out into the world.

It also helps to be able to sense when things are getting static, slow, complicated, to recognize when it's time for a change, and to do something about it.

Like I should have when my parents said no to my artistic dreams or when my studies stalled.

And it's important to say yes when the energy is right, even if you don't know where it will lead you.

Like when I said yes to Bérard even though I could have ignored that weird call. Or when I started working on my blog for nothing else but the passion and the energy.

Because life is short, and fascinating. And, really, there is no time to lose. ✗

At the Shows

Follow me to Planet Fashion Week.
A glamorous, yet crazy world unto itself…

*So I worked worked worked to put my career on track,
took risks, and followed the energy.*
And that's how one day I found myself sitting in the
front row at Paris Fashion Week, which is
kind of the ultimate fashion-industry stamp of approval.

O f course, it all began with standing tickets at small shows. (Okay, sometimes no ticket at all and just a lot of panache, showing up and pretending I had lost my ticket.) But within a few years, I was tensed up next to the toughest editors in the industry, or trying to keep my cool next to the occasional celebrity, at all of the biggest shows.

The thing is, fashion shows are an alternate universe. They're fascinating, draining, and hilarious all at the same time. You want to know what it's like? Here, follow me to the shows. . . .

Let's face it. I lose all perspective when it comes to Fashion Week.

Or Fashion Weeks, I should say.

Because there's New York, followed by London, followed by Milan, followed by Paris . . . Sounds like a dream, right? Right?

This idea—that I might be losing perspective—came to me one day when, after a show, I found myself wondering if it was my duty to rush backstage and throw my arms around the designer.

I had worked with him, we had told each other our life stories, but isn't that what everyone does in the fashion world? Was I now one of the people he would expect to see after the show? Would he be upset if I slipped out early?

In doubt, I joined the frenzied crowd charging the backstage door, and waited for my turn to say hi to a designer already smothered in hugs and congratulations. He seemed ecstatic to see that I was there too . . . I think.

After a moment's hesitation, he called me "darling." That means he recognized me, right?

I wasn't so sure. So I decided to go have a coffee, to get my head straight.

Perhaps I should have chosen a more discreet spot than Le Castiglione on rue Saint-Honoré (during Fashion Week, the only place less private than the runway) for my coffee break. I hadn't even finished ordering when a stylist friend of mine sat down next to me.

"Of course we end up losing our minds! You have champagne for breakfast, you're treated like a princess by some people and like shit by others, and all of that while wearing way-too-high heels.

"You spend all your time making small talk with people you don't even know.

"And after seeing the same faces every day for a month, you can't even remember who you know and end up calling everybody 'darling.'

"On top of that, now we have to tweet.

"Besides, there are only three people a designer wants to see after a show— Suzy, Cathy, and Emmanuelle. Anna comes before the show. And there you are in the middle of it all, like an extra in a movie."

She finally came to the harrowing conclusion:

"Fashion Week isn't what it used to be."

I nodded my head in agreement, but how would I know? My first steps into the fashion world were relatively recent—that is, recent enough for me to realize I'd lost my perspective but not recent enough for me to believe that all of this was perfectly normal.

Without even realizing it, I'd become an insider.

So, what do you do at Fashion Week when you're an insider? Well, first of all, you work. Pfff, boring, I know.

SO, WHO'S WORKING AT FASHION WEEK?

You have the press—the critics giving their opinions on the collections. You have the fashion editors, who are there to find inspiration for their next magazine editorials.

You have the buyers and retailers, who are there to decide what will be in their stores next season (very important, the buyers). Most of the time, they read the critics' advice carefully to get the scoop on what to buy for next year, and then they end up buying the exact same thing they bought the year before.

And, of course, there are the photographers, publicists, makeup artists, designers, and models who work like crazy to make the fashion shows happen.

THEN THERE ARE THE PEOPLE WHO WORK A LITTLE LESS.

There are the starlets (or maybe we're supposed to say "it-girls"), whose job is to be photographed at fashion shows. Depending on the brand they're representing, they embody the young and happy woman or the young and sexy woman.

It's easy to get an it-girl in your front row, even if nowadays:

"Pfff, they all have agents, it's impossible to get them at a show!" or, "Pfffff, everyone is so over those girls, we see them all the time, enough with the it-girls!"

And then there are the celebrities, who are there to:

1. Have their photo taken, if their career is on its way down.

2. Have their photo taken and support the brand that is paying them a LOT of money to be their muse, if their career is on its way up.

3. See the show, if they are interested in fashion. A few are.
I'm not kidding.

But above all, celebrities love going to fashion shows because it's a rare opportunity to get mistreated a little. They get pushed around trying to get through the door, they have to wait forty-five minutes for the show to start, they get too warm and no one even offers them a drink, and, most of all, no one recognizes them.

Because fashion people would never be caught dead recognizing a celebrity. Are you crazy?

Besides, people in the fashion world live (as mentioned) in a parallel universe, so it might actually be the case that they don't recognize Rihanna sitting next to them.

For a celebrity fresh out of that sunny, servile bubble known as Hollywood, going to a fashion show is a liberating experience.

But, as we've covered, *who cares about celebrities?* Let's get back to the shows.

A fashion show is first and foremost a place where people work. The rest is just survival.

GETTING DRESSED: **IT'S ALL RELATIVE.**

As a wise friend once put it: "It's a trap! Even if I don't feel like dressing up to go to a show and I decide to be cool about it, everyone is going to think I actually tried and will say, 'That's the best she can do?'"

So even if you have the most innate sense of style, you still have to make an effort. You must drag three fifty-pound suitcases across Europe, you must make impulsive last-minute purchases (I *must have* the Jil Sander veiled knit hat!), and no matter what you do, you never feel like it's good enough.

GETTING AROUND: **AN EXERCISE IN STYLE.**

You can hire a chauffeur (pros: the mystery of tinted windows, graciously stepping out of the backseat, hosting a party in the back of your Mercedes; cons: never-ending traffic jams), or take a bike (pros: street cred and athletic calves; cons: vulnerability to the elements and permanent bad-hair day), or take a taxi, but good luck finding one in Milan and Paris.

As for the metro, if you are capable of enduring a traumatic plunge into reality between a Lanvin show and a coffee with Anna Dello Russo, then go for it.

GETTING INVITED: **A COMPLEX MATHEMATICAL EQUATION.**

Especially now that the trend is to have fashion shows where no one is invited.

Not to worry: The enormous, spectacular, grandiose, unforgettable, majestic fashion shows still exist.

LOUIS VUITTON

my fashion

JENNA LYONS

WITH LOVE JENNA

MIU MIU

Garance Doré

CHANEL
SHOPPING
C

week clutter

invites
metro tickets
hotel keys
makeup
glasses
notebooks

But you will also see the fashion world reacting to the transformation of Fashion Week into an over-publicized mega-event by curling in on itself and whispering words like "exclusive, secret, inaccessible!" and drastically reducing guest lists. To, like, five people.

"I knew it!" cry out the happy few upon receiving their invitation for Balenciaga one hour before the show.

"Oh no! I'm not going to be able to make it; too bad, I have an important meeting scheduled then," say the others (who weren't invited).

Nobody has an important meeting during the Balenciaga show.

SITTING DOWN: A QUESTION OF VALUES.

Getting an invitation is great, but that's not all. You have to get a seat in the front row. It's kind of like the metro. You'd really like to have a seat, but you'll pretend like you're just fine standing up.

Ah, the front row. The spot where you get photographed, looked at, and wooed. Where the first-class gossip gets traded AND where you can experience the intense satisfaction of rubbing shoulders with celebrities.

Literally: sitting next to Rihanna.

On a side note, it's also the best place to see the clothes. But, don't worry, if you missed everything because you spent ten minutes trying to take a picture of Rihanna's manicure without her noticing, you can make up for it on the Internet as soon as the show ends.

It's already online for the world to see.

COMMUNICATING WITH 140 CHARACTERS: A SKILL YOU NEVER THOUGHT YOU'D NEED.

These days, someone puts a phone in your hand and says, "Now you tweet, you Instagram, you socialize, or you die."

It may be for your newspaper, if you're a journalist; for your store, if you're a buyer; or it may just be your sixth sense, if you are under twenty-five.

In any case, don't make yourself crazy. Do as I do—tweet complete emptiness.

EATING: WHY NOT?

The idea is to eat when you can.

Eating isn't a very interesting subject during Fashion Week.

GOING OUT: I'D LOVE TO.

They say that people who work during Fashion Week don't have time to go out, and it's true. You spend your nights finishing up articles, placing your orders, editing your photos. That's probably why the people who work less are there. They keep the party going and annoy you with their enthusiastic tweets.

If I could, I would go out every night during Fashion Week. Have you guys seen *Vogue*'s party photos?

Amazing!

But you want to know the truth about my Fashion Week evenings? The truth is: room service.

NOT ATTENDING: THE BEST WAY TO GET YOUR PERSPECTIVE BACK.

A concept that's spreading like a cloud of face powder: Fashion Week by proxy.

A friend of mine first discovered this when she was very pregnant during one Fashion Week and couldn't go to the shows. She sat down in front of her computer with a chai latte, got on all the fashion sites, logged onto Twitter, Instagram, and YouTube, and her conclusion was:

"I saw everything. I know exactly what happened. I saw all the shows, even Céline, live. I knew what people thought about the collections right away. I knew which party was great, who was going out with whom, and I was even able to see everything that was going on in the showrooms. It was great. Usually I don't even have the time to see a quarter of what I saw online!"

I guess today the real insider is out. ✕

24h

IN THE LIFE OF GARANCE DORÉ
FREELANCER, ENTREPRENEUR, BOSS

2007

I'm a freelancer, so I work from home. How else to explain why I blog at the weirdest hours of the day?

7h00 — Lucky for me, my cat is an early riser. At the crack of dawn, my ~~fat~~ gracious, hungry feline pulls me out of bed. I throw on ~~old sweat~~ ~~pants~~ a cool and casual outfit, drink ~~an espresso~~ water with lemon, and make a nice little breakfast while ~~looking for friends on Facebook~~ reading *Le Monde*.

9h30 — After ~~pillaging the magazine rack down the block~~ my yoga class, I ~~fall asleep in the bath~~ take an enlivening shower; right after that, I'm ready to look ~~through some~~ ~~blogs~~ at my planner. Four hours later, ~~totally guilt ridden~~ with a sense of accomplishment, I make a few phone calls.

13h30 — This is usually when I like to start putting together ~~some pasta~~ steamed vegetables for lunch that I'll enjoy with ~~the TV on~~ a few friends. A quick ~~nap~~ coffee and then back to work.

Afternoons are my favorite. Everything is calm, and it's the perfect time to ~~go shopping~~ get going on some bigger projects. Time flies ~~in department stores~~ when you're really focused.

18h00 — ~~Panic sets in~~ It's time to take a break. I make some tea that I like to have with ~~a box of cookies~~ an apple. Then it's back to work for an hour or two, just to ~~stop~~ ~~feeling so guilty~~ finish up a few projects.

20h15 — My man is on his way home and the end of the day is near. I'm exhausted, but I have to do some networking ~~at the Flore~~ at a fabulous gala.

23h00 — I get home ~~totally drunk~~ enchanted after this incredibly productive day, ready to start fresh the next.

The life of a freelancer is so hard.

2012

I'm a freelan . . . an entrepreneur. Okay, I'd like to think that I'm still a freelancer, but I have to admit that things have changed quite a bit. So let's update and take a look at my schedule from 2012.

6h30 — I wake up early. I hear my iPhone alarm ~~forty-five minutes after~~ ~~it started~~ at the first ringtone, hop out of bed, and pull on ~~the same~~ ~~sweatpants from 2007~~ my yoga outfit.

Right after I ~~take a quick look at Twitter~~ drink a big glass of water, I do my daily forty-five minutes of ~~reading the ingredients on the back of the box of oatmeal~~ yoga and meditation.

8h45 — My employees are about to arrive. My living space is about to transform into my working space. Time to put my best foot forward and get ready to lead my team by example. I ~~keep daydreaming while looking at Tumblr~~ hop into the shower and think about the super-chic outfit that I'll slip into for my role as inspiring-yet-friendly boss.

9h00—I'm ~~still in my sweatpants~~ on the starting blocks. Emily, my assistant, arrives with a big smile and her Starbucks mug and reminds me that I have a meeting.

Ah, ~~shit!~~ Awesome! I ~~totally forgot~~ am totally ready: looking my best ~~with the first clothes I see in my closet~~ in an outfit that's perfect for a spokeswoman such as myself, perfect hair ~~in knots~~ brushed and ready, PowerPoint that Emily prepared for me and that I ~~of course will forget on her desk~~ know by heart, and off I go into the new and exciting day.

Whether I'm shooting, in a meeting, or ~~chugging a hot chocolate in the~~ ~~kitchen that's dangerously close to my~~ ~~work space~~ brainstorming, I'm super productive.

13h00 — Ooooh, it's time for lunch. Everyone knows that when you're a career woman, you have to use every lunch

to network. So every day I lunch with ~~my boyfriend~~ someone different, just to keep filling my ~~belly~~ address book.

After lunch, I make my way back to the studio. Oh, did I mention? I don't have a desk. Nooope, I'm too ~~disorganized~~ creative for that.

I work ~~sprawled out on my couch~~ wherever inspiration leads me. Everyone at the studio finds it super ~~annoying~~ inspiring.

They love to find traces of ~~my total mess~~ my creative process strewn about everywhere. Hard drives, jump drives, drawing pads . . . With me, you never know when ~~you're going to slip on one of my art pens~~ I'm going to blow your mind with my art.

16h00 — I start ~~freaking out because I haven't even started my post for the next day~~ getting organized to have a meeting on one of my many projects. I'm always super ~~last-minute~~ ahead of schedule with my blog, and that makes me as ~~tense~~ zen as can be.

To get my energy up, like all New Yorkers, I'm a big fan of ~~the cookies from The Grey Dog (five hundred calories)~~ green tea.

19h30 — Everyone is still at the studio and I start trying to shoo my employees out. It takes them about a half hour. I don't know why they love lingering at the office so much, but maybe it has something to do with the ~~meltdowns~~ calming energy that I communicate throughout the day finally taking effect.

I remind them that ~~I~~ they all have lives, that even if they love what they do, going out helps to keep you connected with the pulse of the world around you.

That said, I close the door behind them, hop into my boyfriend's arms, and put on a movie, perfectly chill and totally ~~oblivious~~ connected to the pulse of the world around me.

2015

Garance Doré, Founder, Creative Director, President.
Don't you love my titles? I just gave them to myself.

I've come a long way in my professional life—even though deep down I still can't believe I have my own studio and a team working with me. But it's true; I have seven employees, three agents, two lawyers, and a real studio. I have overhead, guys. So my daily life has changed. Here's how I roll in 2015. . . .

7h30 — I wake up ~~in a crazy rush~~ very early in the morning. Usually I set my alarm for 6:30 ~~and it rings till 8~~ to meet with my ~~huge pot of~~ ~~coffee and tartines~~ personal trainer. It's so important to make time to ~~scroll though Pinterest~~ stay in shape when you have professional responsibilities!

Then I jump into the shower, put on ~~the same jeans and T shirt I was wearing yesterday~~ a simple yet elegant outfit, and head to the studio to get there ~~two hours late~~ before the rest of my team. It's the perfect time of day for ~~a deep chat about what's new on Net A Porter with my sister~~ getting work done. I check my ~~Instagram~~ e-mail, my ~~Twitter~~ schedule, and catch up with the team to discuss ~~Gwyneth Paltrow~~ the plan for the day.

11h00 — Ouch, the morning flies by ~~when you start at 11~~ when you're focused. By now I'm starving, so I ~~eat my team's snacks~~ order my lunch in advance. Then I take a break to ~~have my fifteenth coffee of the day~~ meditate for five minutes in my office. I love it 'cause it's bright and ~~totally messy~~ super minimalist.

11h10 — I'm back in business, and it's time for appointments. I usually pick my outfits for the day ~~straight from our fashion closet~~ in the morning and ~~forget them at my apartment~~ bring them to work. It's ~~impossible to get organized~~ so great to finally have some boundaries between my life and my work!

14h05 — My afternoons are all pretty different; I can be on a shoot, in meetings, illustrating on my computer. Sometimes I also give talks, but my favorite thing in the world is to ~~sleep on the studio couch~~ prepare for our editorial meetings.

16h00 — Editorial meeting begins. These meetings are important, which is why I like them to be ~~a time for talking about whatever is on my mind~~ focused and ~~as short or long as inspiration is with us~~ on time. We always have some ~~macaroons, banana quinoa muffins, and salted chocolate cookies from The Smile~~ fruits and healthy juices on hand for fuel.

When we get short on ideas, we love to ~~open a bottle of wine~~ brainstorm.

I don't know how my team can keep up with my ~~mess~~ passion for my work, but they do. Whenever they get stuck, they know they can come to me for ~~distraction~~ advice. I'm always the one ~~to invade their personal space, start a dance party, and tell them to not stay too late at the~~ ~~office~~ who puts the whole team right on track.

19h00 — We're done, so it's time to ~~walk back home with Beyoncé in my ears~~ jump back into my heels and go for a drink. I like to use my evenings to ~~watch twelve *Game of Thrones* episodes in a row~~ meet people and create synergies. That's how ~~others~~ I roll in New York!

22h15 — After a long day, I ~~finish a pint of Ben & Jerry's~~ sit and do some meditation before going to bed. Maybe that's why I wake up feeling so ~~bloated~~ fresh and ready to ~~kick my alarm clock in the face~~ conquer the world.

My Nomad Office

This is everything I need to work wherever I am — on an airplane, on the
beach, in a car . . . . As long as there's an internet connection, I'm good to go.
With my tablet I can illustrate straight into my computer and then publish to
my blog. I always carry my camera and a little boom box to listen to music. I
do most of my writing on my iPad, but my computer is still the one place where
it all comes together. Optional but appreciated: my watercolors, good earplugs
(I love music when I illustrate, but I can't write with noise), notebooks, and
the books that inspire me when I'm lost in front of a white page.
Oh, and dark chocolate, of course!

ON CAREER

ONE ON ONE WITH A WOMAN WHO INSPIRES ME

Diane von Furstenberg

GD: I'm fascinated by the way you lead your career and your life. How did you get your start?

DVF: I did not always know what I wanted to do, but I knew very, very early that I wanted to be a woman who was independent, who was in charge of her life, who could pay her bills, and who did not depend on a man. The man would be a choice.

GD: How important for you is what people think?

DVF: The most important opinion is your own. The most important relationship you have in your life is the one you have with yourself. If you have that, then any other relationship is a plus and not a must.

GD: How do you deal with difficult moments, where you feel like something you've done was a failure?

DVF: When you are at your lowest, it's probably the most interesting time, because that's when you put yourself in question and you re-invent things.

GD: Do you ask for advice?

DVF: I ask and then I don't listen. (Laughs.)

GD: What would you tell a woman trying to build her career?

DVF: First of all, identify what you're good at. Then go for it. You should be serious about it. But you cannot be narrow-minded. Always be open to new things and new people. That's the beauty of life, and life goes so quickly.

THINGS NEW YORKERS DO

So much has happened in the five years since I moved to New York.
I've learned to navigate the New York City subway,
I've unlearned how to speak French, I've learned to massage kale
(yes, that's what you're supposed to do!), and I have come to
observe (and, of course, make fun of) some New Yorker habits,
before realizing that I've joined their ranks myself.

Yes, I confess, there are...

THINGS NEW YORKERS DO THAT I DO.

× Fighting over cabs. Yelling at a cab because he didn't stop yet had his light on. Threatening someone who is trying to steal *your* taxi. Throwing some colorful insults at the dirty thief and getting the thumbs-up from everyone on the street. Ending up on the subway.

× Thinking, The New York subway, it's pretty nice! I should take it more often!

× Living with a to-go cup of coffee permanently attached to your hand.

× Having your own super-specific coffee order. Mine? Tall latte with a half shot. And no one looks at me weird when I order it.

× Planning on working out every day, never making it to the gym, feeling super guilty, ending up drinking tequila at a bar with your friends to get over your guilt while cursing the impossible standards New York forces us all to try to live up to.

× Talking about healthy food, eating macrobiotic, and colonics, all while devouring a burger at Black Market because it's the BDBNY (the Best Damn Burger in New York).

× Being adamant that you know the true BDBNY.

× Ordering EVERYTHING. Breakfast, lunch, dinner, coffee, wine, shopping, clothes, weed, sex, love, movies. Ordering ANYTHING anytime.

× Saying, "I'm going on a yoga retreat."

× Saying, "I can't sign any contracts this week because Mercury is in retrograde."

× Saying, "I'm looking for a healer. Do you know a good healer?"

× Using "Oh my God" to open or conclude any sentence and to express sadness, joy, surprise, anger, boredom, and pleasure. *Oh my God,* yes!

× Saying, "Oh my God, we haaaaave to get coffee sometime!!!!" and then never ever getting in touch.

- Wearing sweatpants for every occasion—to go to the gym, to take your dog for a walk, to run to the deli, to go to the spa, to head nowhere at all, to meet friends for brunch (but make everyone think you're coming from the gym—pick a good pink blush for this). Point is, sweatpants, everywhere, all the time.

- Almost losing your sh#t because you just realized that the dinner you said yes to is in BROOKLYN.

- Not seeing your friends for months, even though you live on the same street, and bitching about how everyone is too busy. Then hearing yourself say, "Dinner? Yes, of course! How does three weeks from now sound to you?"

- Spending three weeks planning said dinner, sending a thousand e-mails to get four fu#*ing friends together, then an hour on the phone with the restaurant to get a good table at a decent hour (okay, any table. Okay, 9:30). And then . . .

- Canceling at 9:27 because "Oh my God, I'm so exhausted. Would you be upset if I . . ."

- Being totally blasé when you say, "Look, Cameron Diaz is seated at the table behind you." "Oh, so annoying, they're shooting *Girls* on my street again." "Yeah, there were tons of paparazzi by my house today."

- Being in a good mood all the time. Smiling, talking to strangers in the street, being super friendly, holding the door open, and being generally very well behaved, *unless some asshole is trying to steal your taxi.*

- Never carrying cash and HAVING NO IDEA WHAT TO DO WITH YOURSELF if some shop only takes cash. "What? Cash? What's that? How? Why?"

- Hugging everyone like you're best friends that haven't seen each other for years, even if it's only the third time you've met.

- Saying, "OMG, I LOVE YOU," to someone you think is nice.

- Saying, "Seriously, that guy? He's a modelizer."

- Taking two years to say, "I really like you," to the guy you love.

- Being super excited about pretty much everything, working all the time, always having a new project, doing seventy-five different things at the same time yet still thinking that you're not doing enough.

THINGS NEW YORKERS DO THAT I DON'T DO YET, THANK GOD.

- Scheduling a weekend like a back-to-school Monday: 9:00, yoga; 11:00, pre-brunch with friends; 1:00, brunch with your love; 3:00, mani-pedi with your best friend; 5:00, run all over town to figure out what you're going to wear for dinner; 6:30, cocktails; 8:00, dinner; 11:00, head out dancing.

- The next day, pick different people, different places and do it all over again.

(Personally, I'm much more into having no plans at all, then finding some friends and hanging out for as long as possible with nothing on the agenda. Sometimes, if I stay too long, my New York friends start to think I'm weird. I just say: "I'm not weird, I'm French.")

× Having lunch in front of your computer at work.

× Working until 2:00 a.m. without complaining because that's the price you pay for having a "creative" job. Okay, complaining a little, just for the pleasure of it.

× Swearing by Soul Cycle, Ballet Beautiful, or Physique 57, three different workouts that supposedly give you long lean muscles and that are known for their difficulty, their exorbitant prices, and the impossibility of finding a spot in class. "Yeah, yeah, what you're saying is true, Garance, but you have to try it! It changed my life! I'm addicted!"

× Having a dog and someone to walk it. Or putting your dog in doggie day care, where he can "spend time socializing and playing with other dogs" (yes, "socializing" is now a word for dogs) instead of just waiting for you to come home. It's so much better!

× Throwing down ten thousand dollars per year on a trainer and justifying the expense by saying that if you're in awesome shape, you'll spend less on clothes, which is completely false.

× Enduring the weekend ritual of Holy Sacred Brunch, where you have to shout to hear anyone, throw elbows to find a menu that only offers eggs anyway, and where the bill's on the table before you've had the chance to put your fork back on your plate. Doing it all again the following weekend.

× Pretending you're enthralled by the conversation you're having with a fellow party guest while scanning the room to decide which person you're going to say hello to next.

× Going on vacation to Tulum, or the Hamptons, or upstate, to "get away from the stress of New York life." Then realizing that all of New York had the same idea and finding yourself at a work dinner while on vacation, with the same people from New York but a little more tan and a little more drunk. Complain together about life in NYC.

Coming back and shedding a tear the first time you see the Empire State Building through the window of the plane. Instagramming from the plane, because who cares about scrambling signals? New Yorkers know that scrambling signals is a myth, because they're smart like that. Posting #NewYorkI LoveYou.

Yes, New Yorkers are crazy and hilarious. But don't make too much fun: I feel like one of them already. Guess what one of the favorite New Yorker pastimes is?

Talking about being a New Yorker. ✕

Beauty

Whatever is gi
on the day you
you are the one u
who you will b
every day. *Beau*
we grow into o

n to you

re born,

o decides

come,

grows as

rselves.

Growing beautiful

Growing up, I was not the pretty one.
Or let's say I was the pretty one—until the day my
younger sister, Laetitia, became devastatingly gorgeous.

I was about fourteen, and Laetitia, who had been a funny-faced, long-limbed, scruffy tween, turned into a fantastic beauty overnight. What a tough moment for a teenager—I even remember plotting to shave her head while she slept. Good thing I never got up the nerve. Instead, I lived and I learned . . .

. . . THAT BEAUTY MAKES PEOPLE CRAZY.

There she was, tall and slim with full lips, a tiny, delicate nose, and big, wide eyes. She had perfect teeth, and even her toes, I thought, had a much better shape than mine.

It was fascinating to see the effect on people. Out of nowhere, photographers wanted to take her picture. She received flowers at home from men who had only seen her walk down the street. And, of course, people started to say she should be a model.

I remember it all so well, because I agonized through every moment, as only a teenager can.

I had always been incredibly cherished in my family—possibly a little spoiled—and in the blink of an eye, I was a mess of hormones; I developed acne and put on weight. And I had a crazy-beautiful sister that no one could stop talking about. I felt myself disappearing in the eyes of those around me, and it hurt.

My sister, Laetitia Beveraggi, on the streets of New York City.

You could say the people around me were being insensitive, but I don't think they meant anything by it. I learned that beauty fascinates and intoxicates.

. . . I ALSO LEARNED THAT BEAUTY IS RELATIVE.

If not for my sister, I might have gone on living as if I was a great beauty, who knows? I might never have known how it felt to lose my parents' unconditional adoration. To me, a dramatic teenager, it felt like a fall from grace.

You have to forgive my parents. Part of it was that they saw a future for my sister—she didn't like school much, whereas I had always been the one with good grades. In a few months' span, I had become the smart one and she was the beautiful one, which was as insulting and diminishing to her as it was to me.

But that's what happens with beauty. Depending on who's around, you can be the most amazing creature in the room. Or not worth raising an eye at. I've seen it happen with models, poor little things thrown into the big scary fashion world, where there will always be someone more perfect or more beautiful.

But at the time, things just seemed easier when I stayed away from my sister. So I did, and we grew apart. Unfortunately for her, I was not the only one. She had a tough time finding and keeping friends.

. . . I LEARNED THAT BEAUTY CAN MAKE YOU SUFFER.

People are often as repulsed as they are attracted by beauty.

My sister was not what you might imagine. At fifteen she decided that she was not interested in modeling and that everybody should leave her alone. That put the brakes on the drama of photo shoots and meetings at modeling agencies every weekend.

She never talked again about it. She really didn't care.

She loved fashion, though, and grew into an incredibly stylish woman, and everywhere she goes, she makes heads turn.

And as thrilling as those adoring looks can be (I know, I live vicariously through my sister very frequently), it's not easy.

It makes relationships with people complicated. Beauty is blinding, and it takes depth and intelligence to see through it to the real person beneath.

The danger is that if you make beauty the focus of your life, you attract people who do the same.

. . . BEAUTY IS NOT THAT IMPORTANT.

You live and you learn. As an adult, I reconnected with my sister, who turned out to be a warm, smart, honest, wonderful, and happy person. Today she is my best and closest friend in the world. Through her, I saw some of the complications and pitfalls beauty can bring to a life.

I finally stopped envying her beauty and started liking my flaws. I came to recognize my own type of beauty, began seeing myself as whole, and I found that I am more inspired by women who make life exciting than by perfect plastic beauty.

I also realized that looks have absolutely no correlation to the quality and the beauty of the life you create.

Beauty, as it turned out, was not that important.

Because the thing is, whatever is given to you on the day you are born, you are the one who decides who you will become, every day. Beauty grows as we grow into ourselves.

My beautiful sister managed to become a deeply profound, strong woman in spite of the false dreams people threw at her.

Laetitia and I have both grown to embrace this truth as we age and as beauty becomes more about what we've made of ourselves and less about what we were given.

Oh, and I almost forgot to tell you.

Today, with her compassion, love, and infinite admiration, my sister is the one who makes me feel like the most beautiful person in the world. ✕

The Mirror

I was with a friend, walking around
Bed Bath & Beyond—I know, so glamorous—
when suddenly I heard her cry out.

"Aaaaaah! Emergency!!! Tell me that's not me!"

Right there in front of her was a magnifying mirror framed by a bright light-up ring to illuminate your face. I walked up carefully behind her and, as I got closer, I saw the reflection of my own nose cross the mirror like the Starship *Enterprise*.

"Oooooh my God. What is this thing?!? My nose is huge. My freckles look like corn-flakes. AND I'VE GOT A WRINKLE ON MY CHIN!!! Where did that come from? I didn't even know that could exist!"

"Seriously, do you see my pores?!!! My skin is like the moon! There are craters everywhere!!! Oh my God. Hold my hands. Let's cry."

"Heeeeey, wait wait wait, I see something. Hold on, you've got a hair there. See it in the mirror? Wait, don't move. I think I have some tweezers in my bag. Oh my goodness, it's HUGE! It's like a tree trunk! Come here, turn toward me. . . . Well, now I don't see it anymore. Wait, go look in the mirror again."

"Aaaaaaaah! Help! Help! The tree trunk has returned."

"Okay. Pinpointed its coordinates. Turn toward me. . . . Bahhh, it disappeared again."

"Actually, ummm, Garance, I don't see your chin wrinkle at all. I did see it in the mirror. But now it's gone. With the naked eye, honestly, there's nothing there. . . . So what do we do here?"

"We buy this thing, right?"

"OF COURSE."

You know, it's just way too easy being happy with yourself. ✗

Constance Jablonski

How to look better in a Photo

I'm the opposite of photogenic.
The camera hates me, which is upsetting because I love
her very much. Love hurts, I'm telling you.

No, shhhhhh, don't argue. I didn't say I'm ugly. I know I'm hot. I'm just saying I'm not photogenic.

That's the way it is. Some people capture the light perfectly right; others don't.

That's why a girl can look amazing in a photo but only so-so in real life, or the opposite. Ugly in photos, sublime in day-to-day life. One percent of us are beautiful in both, and that's because there is no justice in the world.

I used to think that being un-photogenic was my fate, just a fact of life, but it's not. Here are some of the tricks I've been forced to figure out, growing tired of looking at pictures of myself and thinking Oh, look, I look like my grandma here! Oh, and here I look like Marlon Brando in *The Godfather*!

USE NATURAL LIGHT.

Light used well is like natural Photoshop.

When you're inside, always stand facing the window, in front of the light. It will erase everything from wrinkles to acne to bags under your eyes.

But be careful: Inside or outside, don't go in direct sunlight. It will cast intense, rough shadows and make your face a Picasso. So find a spot where the light is a little more moderate or wait for the sunset's soft light.

At night or with no natural light available, all bets are off, because everything depends on your camera. Just try to control what you can, and . . .

POWDER YOUR NOSE.

Pat McGrath is the only one who can make dewy skin look good in pictures. If you have shiny skin, grab a tissue and tap it on your T zone. It's simple and it works.

Dark lipstick isn't always great for photos; it can give a pinched look. Transparent lip gloss, on the other hand, is perfect; it plumps and freshens. *Vive le* lip gloss!

The smoky eye is a miracle that widens the eye and works on everyone. And that's great because photos tend to make eyes look smaller.

Lastly, moisturize! Legs, arms, hands, feet . . . We always do this on fashion shoots, and it changes everything. My favorite lotion for a perfectly voluptuous shine is Kiehl's Creme de Corps.

BE A POSER.

Do you know Ulyana Sergeenko, the Russian it-girl/designer who struts around the shows as if the world is her catwalk? It's okay if you don't; you can imagine—she'll work the same pose for hours, and, honestly, sometimes it gets close to ridiculous.

Yes, *but*. All the photos of her are perfect.

To translate to real life, let's just say it doesn't hurt to figure out and master a few poses that make you look good.

This page: Isabel Wilker
Opposite: Lauren Bastide

KNOW YOUR GOOD SIDE.

We all have one. Knowing it changes EVERYTHING.

Ask a friend to take a few pictures with your phone to help you figure it out, because it's impossible to tell with a mirror. Once you've figured it out, use and abuse it.

Celebrities do this all the time. When I interview celebrities on video, they won't shy away from saying to me, "Do you mind if I sit on this side instead? It's my good side!" And I don't blame them—it's their job to look good.

I, on the other hand, have to say, "Of course!" and sit with my bad side to the camera. Damn!

ASK YOURSELF:
WHERE IS THE CAMERA?

FULL BODY

If you're standing and the camera is above you, you're gonna get squashed and lose five good inches—so not fair. If it's below you, you look like a scary giant. It's best to have the camera at chest height.

If you're seated, sit up and take your back off the chair.

CLOSE UP

Place the camera a little bit above you and lift your head toward it, which is usually where the light is coming from.

It will hit all the right angles and define your jaw, which also helps with your angles. Very important since the goal in life of the modern woman is to have good angles.

And my number-one piece of advice for good selfies: Look up toward the sun!

PLAY.

Have fun. It's hard to do, but to be beautiful in photos you have to play with the camera a little. Move, laugh, do something silly, make a sexy face.

Un-photogenic people are so used to bad pictures that whenever they see a camera they freeze, which only makes things worse—a vicious cycle.

Try to tap into your emotions, laugh, chat, move, have someone tell you a story.

Play the game, BUT . . .

This page: Wini Burkeman
Opposite: Shala Monroque

LEARN TO SAY NO.

Sometimes, conditions are perfect for a horrible photo.

You've just spent the whole night out, you're exhausted, the light is crappy, you're wearing Big Lebowski clothes, you're sweating, your hair looks like you spent three days at Katz's Delicatessen (a New York institution, where gigantic portions and fried food abound!). Oh well, it's just not your day.

In this case, say no to the photo. Simple as that.

It's tough, I know. I could never say no to a photo at first. We all want to please others and end up saying to ourselves, Oh, pffff, who cares if I look ugly in photos?! And then we have to spend hours untagging bad pictures and praying no one will recognize us.

Okay, if you really can't say no, do what the fashion editors do: Put on the biggest sunglasses you can find. Yes, even at night.

What, you really thought it was just to be fashionable? ✕

Long Story Short: my hair

*You should hear my mother and sisters
complain about their curls.*
The drama! The distress! The time spent
battling nature!

The anxiety of humidity, the menace of the roots, the instruments used to tame them.

Curly hair is unruly, rebellious, it takes up so much space—and, also, it has a life of its own. I understand; I silently commiserate.

But I can't really participate.

If I try, I get shushed and they look at me as if I'm mocking them.

You have to understand: In my family, I'm the one with the good hair.

Their locks are dark and curly, the proud heritage of our Mediterranean descent. Unlike my mother's and sisters', which tend to be on the extreme side of the frizz, my curls are soft, manageable, easy to live with.

So I guess you could say I have nice hair—but of course it would be way too boring to sit back and enjoy it. Like every woman in this world, I want Gisele Bündchen hair (okay, I'd take Gisele Bündchen anything), meaning: beach curls, soft highlights, French messiness, all together on ~~my~~ a gorgeous face.

Embracing what Mother Nature gave me? Who does that? Not me. I've tried everything.

I TRIED TO ACCEPT MY HAIR.

"What's wrong with luscious curls?" I hear you say.

Well, after years of studying photos of Andie MacDowell and trying to rock the curl, I've realized that when I set my hair free, it takes over.

My features get eaten up by the volume, and, also, hair gets in my face. It tickles my skin like a bad mohair sweater, and as a result it always ends up in a bun.

Embracing my curls? Maybe in a next life.

I TRIED TO EMBRACE THE BUN.

A bun, and especially a topknot, is great. You pull everything up, even your face comes with it. Which is, approaching forty, not a terrible side effect, right?

A friend even told me once: "You're a hair-up girl, that's how you look best. That's it! Accept it."

I went with it, and it became my signature look for about two years. Until one day I started noticing some broken hair. (Having your hair up all the time is terrible for the scalp. It causes traction alopecia and can permanently damage your hairline.)

Keeping my hair in such a tight state wasn't making me feel very sensual anyway.

Topknot, you're fired.

I TRIED TO GO OUT WITH THE BLOWOUT.

All my girlfriends do it. Why not me?

So I learned to blow-dry my hair to turn my wild curls into dreamy beach waves.

Well, I'm sorry to report that I simply can't do it. I'm not coordinated enough to do anything behind my back. I get lost in the movement. I burn my face.

Also, blow-drying makes me sweat and I want to throw myself in the shower, undoing all that I've accomplished over the four hours I just spent swearing in front of my mirror.

So, blow-dryers and flat irons, the door is that way.

I TRIED TO USE CHEMICAL WEAPONS.

I had a keratin treatment and IT WORKED. Miracle of miracles!!!

I found myself with Gisele's hair, or a close enough approximation that I could have lived with it, if only I had known before I spent five hundred dollars and four hours breathing chemicals that, no matter what I do, I still prefer my hair off my face. Even Gisele-d, I just can't be bothered.

FINALLY, WITH NOTHING TO LOSE, I DECIDED TO GO SHORT.

I did a lot of research and found Clyde, a wonderful hairdresser whose salon was close to me. I knew that with short hair, you have to get ready to spend a lot of time with your hairdresser.

Then I made a folder with all the short hairstyles I liked.

I also added those I didn't like, of course. I ended up with about a hundred photos. Yes, Michelle Williams, you were there. Yes, Jean Seberg, you were too. Keri Russell with short curly hair, you were there, but in the lefthand column, if you know what I mean.

Looking at all the photos, I realized three things.

Short hair can look good on any type of face.

There are as many short styles as there are long.

If everything goes wrong? Hair grows back.

I showed my inspiration folder to some friends. I have to report that I didn't get so much support from them. Change is scary.

Here is a recap of their texts:

× "G, we gotta talk." (most people)

× "I'm worried about the soccer-mom look." (From a friend who's a former cheerleader)

× "I'd worry about the texture. With your frizzy hair, it might take over your head." (From a friend with a perpetual ponytail)

× "Whatever you decide, you're beautiful; anything would work on you. Beauty comes from the inside." (From my mother; love you, Mom!)

It was too late anyway; my decision was made. I was ready, even if it was a mistake. I needed to know. Was I living a life that was not my own? (And by that I mean, was I trapped in the life of a long-haired girl when I was actually supposed to be a short-haired girl?)

That's how one day I took a ~~double-margarita~~ deep breath and headed off to see Clyde.

We had a long chat.

We were both a little bit worried about short curly hair. How would it behave?

After long hours spent studying photos, I had decided to ask Clyde to leave some length in the front. That way the haircut would be more versatile—leaving me with the option of blowing it out a bit in the front if I needed to.

And just like that, Clyde started cutting. I went silent.

As my hair hit the floor, I almost felt like my past was gathering at my feet. I was freaked out and very quiet at the same time. Going short is a pretty cathartic experience. I hadn't really thought about it, but I found myself close to tears.

It took a long time, because we went in increments, but gradually, my face started brightening, my features getting more defined. I felt lighter and daring, inside and out.

A few hours later, I was on my way to the café where I had planned to meet a friend, feeling so weird and undecided—I was walking with my head down, trying to catch my reflection in windows, worried and febrile. . . . Who was this new girl I was going to be?

My friend saw me, and I read on her face immediately that it was going to be okay. She loved it. As for me, it took me three days to get used to it.

I've had short hair for more than a year now and I am still incredibly happy about it.

It definitely changed my life; it's easy, different, and I get compliments on it all the time. My hair adapted so well to the cut that I don't even have to straighten it. Combing it and letting it dry naturally works wonders. My mom and sisters hate me!

I did have to change a few things in the way I dress (that's called a shopping opportunity), and I cannot go out without makeup (that's called politeness).

When I look at old pictures of me with long hair, I barely recognize myself. I guess I *was* trapped in the life of a long-haired girl. It just took me some time to set the short-haired girl free. ✗

WAS I LIVING A LIFE THAT WAS NOT MY OWN?

(AND BY THAT I MEAN, WAS I TRAPPED IN THE LIFE OF A LONG-HAIRED GIRL WHEN I WAS ACTUALLY SUPPOSED TO BE A SHORT-HAIRED GIRL?)

MY BEAUTY ESSENTIALS

Beauty really comes from the inside, though a little makeup always helps. We are all so different, and what works for me won't necessarily work for you. But I rely on trial and error, and draw inspiration from the beautiful women around me. These are my essentials. I hope that they inspire you.

the Red lip

The red lip is an accessory I add when I feel like my outfit needs extra sparkle, or when I want to make it a special day, or night. The tricky part is keeping lipstick in check throughout the day — so I always carry a little mirror with me.

MY BEAUTY ESSENTIALS

the Bronzer

On days when you want to feel bright and glowy, a bronzer
works wonders. My secret? Accent the cheeks, chin, and
forehead, stay minimal everywhere else. Finish with a touch
of bronzer on the eyelids, and put some gloss on your lips.
I've used Guerlain Terracota for years. It's very natural
looking and not too sparkly.

Camilla Deterre

the Manicure

I either go clear polish or red. A deeper red for winter
and a bright, coral red for summer. I like my red to look
very fresh, so I only keep it on for a few days. My favorite
polishes are from Essie — somehow the finish is perfect.
The real secret to beautiful hands is hydrated skin, so I
always keep a hydrating balm in my bag.

the blush

Probably my favorite makeup item, for that pink, healthy glow.
It makes anyone instantly more beautiful. I use it and abuse
it. My favorite is from Chanel.

It's funny, the first thing that I discovered upon arriving in New York, apart from its gigantitude and its noise, is that all the women have PERFECTLY MANICURED nails. It put me in a deep state of self-doubt. Where was I trying to go with my chipped nails? Down in the ranks of society?

Having perfect nails takes time, commitment, and money, yet in New York every woman does it. There must be something in the air. Something about being the best you can be, but also giving in to the pressure of perfection. Something . . . a little bit over the top.

Perfectionism is a real lifestyle here. There's a nail spa on every corner, with all the Essie colors of the rainbow at your disposal, and it's quick and relatively cheap. So I had no excuse not to be perfectly put together right up to the cuticle.

Still, it took me some time to adjust.

But eventually I mastered the perfect New York manicure. You need to:

1. LEARN A NEW LANGUAGE.

The first time I walked into a nail spa, I stopped at the desk and I started off at the hostess:

"Hello! I want a manicure, a pedicure, some color, and what's this paraffin thing? Can you take me right away? How long will it take? Can I bring my own polish? What are all those crazy machines over there, and what exactly do you mean by 'facial'? And what do you call that thing that, errrr, I forget; do you think I have good skin? What would you recommend for . . . "

The receptionist stared back at me with wide eyes, a little terrified. After a rather embarrassing two minutes of silence, she started repeating:

"Manicure? Pedicure? Manicure? Pedicure? Manicure? Pedicure? Manicure?"

I looked around, a little lost.

That's when a very pretty and very busy-looking girl blazed into the salon. She picked out a polish in two seconds, put it right in the receptionist's face, and, with no hello but with a big smile, said, "Manicure! Pedicure! Facial!" This was met with a knowing smile, and she was guided into the salon.

And then I finally got it: The receptionist doesn't speak English.

I picked out a polish and said, "Manicure!" And look at that! It worked!

2. BUY A PAIR OF FLIP-FLOPS.
EVEN IF YOU HATE THEM,
GET SOME FLIP-FLOPS.

The second time I went to a nail spa, it was in the middle of winter. This time, I wanted to try a "Pedicure! Manicure!" The only problem was that my feet were trapped in boots, and I got a little worried about how it all would end, when I'd have to get the boots back on without letting the nails dry properly.

With the help of a few huge gestures and hand signs, I signaled the receptionist about my boots. "You have a solution for these?"

"No problem," she said with her thumbs up, and showed me their futuristic drying machines.

And I thought, Pfffff, they have it all in NYC. They even have supersonic nail dryers.

Of course. New Yorkers have thought of it all.

But then when I got back home and saw my new nails totally ruined, I finally understood why, even in the middle of winter, with the crazy snow and all, I had seen New Yorkers walking around, with perfectly manicured nails, IN FLIP-FLOPS.

Bad news. Even in New York, there is no such thing as a supersonic nail dryer.

3. LEARN TO TIP FAST, AND WELL.

The moment will come, in the middle of having your nails done (after the little hand massage but right before the application of the nail polish), when you will have to tip (yeah, you don't want to be looking for money in your bag if you have fresh polish, you fool non–New Yorker).

And right there, girl, you'd better tip. And you'd better tip well. And you'd better tip IN CASH.

Remember, they still have your nail-polish destiny in their hands!

4. ALWAYS REMEMBER.

It's so easy to get addicted to perfection (or nail perfection anyway). You end up going to your salon every week, with the smile of the winner, feeling like such an accomplished New York woman.

But I give you no more than six months to discover that, under your shiny cherry-red manicure, your nails are a war zone.

Because of the buffer that makes them soft, the cuticle cutting that makes your skin rebel, and the chemicals in the nail polish that smother your poor little nails.

I have three solutions for you.

Learn to say: "No buffer! No cut cuticles!"

Learn to do your own manicure. It's so easy! And then when you find yourself on a desert island or, say, in France with no chance of a nail spa on the horizon, who's gonna be the girl with the perfect nails? You, of course.

Learn to take a break from perfect nails once in a while. Try moderation.

Or go completely crazy. Be different. Go bare. ✗

PERFECTION

IS A REAL

LIFESTYLE

HERE.

STORY OF MY ~~LIFE~~
body

As a teenager, I was perfectly fine with my body. I loved exercising. I was a dancer, a swimmer, a windsurfer, a real tomboy; I was more interested in competing with the boys than with the girls.

I left my body alone, which was actually not so easy. At fourteen, like a lot of teenagers, I gained a bit of weight. I personally hadn't noticed it at all, but I can assure you that people around me made sure to point it out.

My mom, who is on a perpetual diet, wouldn't let it go. It was painful— it suddenly put my body into the category of "things I have to worry about if I want to win at life." I went on my first diet. Of course, I failed.

My mom must have seen herself in me—I was the one in the family who had inherited her curves. The problem was that with a few ill-considered words, she had taken me with her on her lifelong crusade against calories.

Had I taken after my father, I would be taller and naturally slender, like my sister and my brother. And maybe I would have had a much simpler relationship with food, as they both do today.

My curves never really bothered me, though. In the grand scheme of things, I was a really healthy girl who loved to move, to dress up and look cool. My boyfriends loved me the way I was, and I laughed about it over endless conversations with my friends, who felt just like I did about their bodies: Who doesn't think they have five pounds to lose?

When I was a teenager, the icons were women like Cindy Crawford and Elle Macpherson, girls with real flesh and bodies, and I could somewhat identify with them. Kate Moss was considered extremely skinny and more interesting-looking than attractive.

I didn't know that this type of body was about to become the new normal.

And also, I love food.

I come from a family of Italian chefs on my father's side (I can cook a fantastic lasagna) and a long line of passionate Moroccan cooks on my mother's side (you should have seen my grandmother preparing couscous. It took her three days). As for my mom, don't judge her about the diet thing—she was an amazing and very modern cook. She cooked vegetables like a queen, and we had the best, most balanced diet at home.

She would fix delicious lunches, simple and healthy (we lived so close to school that my brother, my sister, and I would go back home to eat). And every evening she would prepare a fantastic homemade green soup, with a piece of bread and a yogurt to finish the meal. Special dessert would be a beautiful strawberry salad with a little bit of whipped cream. She taught us to love fresh vegetables and fruits. My dad, being a chef, wouldn't cook at home as much, but when he did, we were in for a treat. He makes the best fondant au chocolat in the world.

In a nutshell, I loved food, I had a pretty good relationship with it, and I was fine with my body the way it was. I simply felt *bien dans ma peau,* as we say.

As I hit my twenties, I lost interest in sports. I took the occasional dance class with my friends (usually spent giggling at the back of the room), but in the exercise department, I'll admit, I couldn't have been more French. On one hand, making an effort to exercise seemed like a pretty incongruous, heroic, bizarre thing. On the other hand, I would walk everywhere, dance all night, lived in a fifth-floor walk-up, and always remembered to tighten my butt cheeks at every step I was taking.

Living on my own for the first time, with roommates or boyfriends, I had time to cook, and was all about fresh, easy, Mediterranean food. Okay, maybe I had an impossible sweet tooth and I couldn't live without my four o'clock tea and cookies and/or chocolate. But all was well. Even as I moved to Paris and felt the pressure mounting.

Parisians with their tall, slim silhouettes. Meh, what could I do?

I had more important things on my plate than thinking about my weight. I needed to figure out how to live in that crazy-expensive city without a euro in my pocket. I might have tried the occasional half-day diet for good measure, failing miserably as usual. But, really, it was nothing to worry about.

And then I moved to New York. All of a sudden I was living in a totally, completely, intensely different culture. The first thing that struck me when I arrived was the complicated relationship many New Yorkers have with food and their bodies. A few months after my move, I was observing and mocking it all.

Seriously! Have you ever had lunch with a New York woman? Even up close, they are fantastically put together, from head to toe, all the way to their nails. They have perfect hair, perfect skin, and their outfits, even if they're vintage, seem brand-new. And they are really, and I mean really, skinny.

Okay, for full disclosure, I should probably say that when I first arrived in New York, the women I met all worked in fashion. Later I met lots of other people, and I can say that not *all* New Yorkers are this way, phew.

But women in fashion in New York, they're not just skinny. They're New York skinny, meaning thin to the brink, yet with super-long, lean muscles from Pilates, Anna Wintour style. Muffin top? Sorry, what?

Have you ever had lunch with Parisians? Well, all right: Have you ever had lunch with me?

Lunch in Paris usually involves a glass of wine, one or two desserts to share; no need for an appetizer, but stuffing your face full of half the bread on the table is totally okay. Finish with a coffee and twelve cigarettes, saying that "No, hehehe, it's no good, oh, but so much fun."

It was cute to be the only Parisian at a table of New Yorkers at first. They would watch me rip off another piece of bread, order a glass of wine and a dessert, and ask me my secret to staying slim despite such a devastating diet.

And I'd just laugh and say that everyone in New York is just too skinny, that they have to live a little, and that, no, I don't work out at all, because I have so many other fascinating things to do with my life.

And also that I'm perfectly fine with my little muffin top, thank you.

This game went on for a little while. It was fun.

Then I started giving in to some of the conveniences of the New York lifestyle. Eating out, ordering in. Never ever cooking. Jumping into cabs and elevators. Walking around with my latte. Snacking at any time of the day.

Until, actually, my muffin top took on a mind all its own. I swear, I couldn't get my skinny jeans to button, aka disaster.

All of a sudden I stopped being so smug at lunch. I had gained weight. And I had gained weight like I'd never gained weight before.

That's when I started to understand some of the big differences between eating in Paris and eating in New York.

THE LIFESTYLE

Yes, Parisians have more fun when they go out. But they're also ten times less likely to eat out. And in Paris, there's no ordering in—you cook. It's simple cooking, really: You can have five friends over, create a fast, delicious pasta with zucchini and mint. Or you just buy cheese, figs, wine, and call it a night.

In New York, your social life happens outside the house. You have meals out. All the time. The only time I had "cooked" since moving to New York was making crepes to show just how French I was.

THE PORTIONS AND THE PACE

In Paris, everybody breaks for lunch. In smaller French cities, people even go back home *entre midi et deux* (between twelve and two) to sit and eat. Whether you have a little salad at the brasserie, or a meal prepared at home and eaten in the park with a few friends, or alone while reading a

I'D JUST LAUGH
AND SAY THAT, NO,
I DON'T WORK OUT
AT ALL, BECAUSE
I HAVE SO MANY
OTHER FASCINATING
THINGS TO DO
IN MY LIFE.

novel, you really take the time to appreciate the break. You eat slowly and consciously.

Imagine my angst when I saw my employees eating in front of their computers. "Hey, guys, there is a table here; please make me happy and eat at the table!" They would look at me with wide eyes. Eating in front of the computer felt like sacrilege to me.

Oh, and the portions—remarkable, like everything in New York. You understand right away the doggie-bag concept that makes everyone laugh in France.

THE FOOD CHAIN

Bigger country, bigger industry. Not to say that everything is perfect in France (it's really not), but the laws on manufactured food are very strict—it's difficult, for example, to find fruits when they're not in season. GMOs are forbidden (we, of course, walked the streets to protest against them), and the label "organic" is extremely tough to obtain. It's not the same in the United States, where it feels more difficult to trust the food you're buying. Hence the success of places like (the extremely expensive) Whole Foods.

These are just a few of the things that can make for a complicated relationship with what you eat—and drive you to extremes. Gluten-free, dairy-free, vegan, Paleo . . .

France is hardly a paradise of health and self-acceptance. We still smoke like chimneys!!! But it's certainly less about extremes, and we don't think that you're either perfect or a total disaster. We're fine with okay.

So there I was, stuck between New York–skinny, my relaxed French attitude, and the pounds that kept adding up behind my boastful smile. And the way I saw myself changed—instead of thinking that these people were skinny, I began to think that I must be the one who was fat. I didn't feel "normal" anymore. I started questioning my lifestyle . . . and looking at myself critically in the mirror.

Stripped naked, we're always beautiful. Our man loves us just the same. And our friends couldn't care less about a few extra pounds. And we really can be just as happy. I mean, really, nothing changes when we get a little plumper.

Okay, that's almost true.

There's that moment when you see a photo of yourself and you suddenly feel like you're about to pass out.

Or the jeans that don't quite button and you pretend to forget them in some dark corner of your closet.

And there's that quiet discomfort. It's hard to explain to the skinny ones, but those few extra pounds . . . You wear them.

I really tried to be cool about it, and the people around me were always very nice: "You look great!" I would smile and joke, "No, look here, I'm fat!" but inside I wasn't feeling that confident. I was just so profoundly annoyed with it all. I knew I had to do something, but I had no idea where to start. That's when something weird happened. I started thinking about food and weight constantly. What I had eaten and what I shouldn't eat, what I was going to eat in the next hour compared with what I had eaten the hour before, and what I should be eating, this instead of that, or that instead of this. All. The. Time.

I would spend all day putting myself down about my weight—not only useless and completely egotistical, but on top of that, I was miserable. And I hate taking myself too seriously. I was not me anymore. I was sad, obsessive, boring, and getting heavier every day. I was in a downward spiral and something had to change.

One night, I broke down. It happened when I was traveling for a shoot in Australia, far from everyone and everything I knew and loved. I looked in the mirror in my lonely hotel room, and my eyes were so sad and empty. I heard a little voice inside me ask, How long is this little game with yourself gonna last? 'Cause this is taking you down, and fast.

I cried it out, called my boyfriend, my best friend, and my shrink, and felt sorry for myself one last time. And then I decided it was over. It's like when you finally decide to quit the job that is killing you or cut ties from that toxic relationship you're in. I had had enough.

I decided to stop intellectualizing everything that passed through my lips and to do what came naturally. I started to do some yoga to help quiet my mind. I also decided to stop speaking to myself negatively and to stop beating myself up about gaining weight. If it was my destiny to become round, well, then why the hell not? I knew tons of amazing people who happened to be curvy. And it wouldn't hurt to have another point of view in the fashion world.

I lived that way for a few months, and it felt better. I had found my smile again. But feeling *bien dans ma peau* with that extra weight proved to be more challenging than I thought it would be. We don't all put on curvies like Christina Hendricks.

Life, you bitch. How was I ever going to get it right? Find a balance?

The answer came to me one day, as I was sitting at the Café de Flore with my very Parisian friend Sophie. We were drinking rosé and I was watching her munch down frite after frite. She was savoring each one, as usual, and as usual her figure was perfect.

I was telling her my life story, and seeing her so relaxed around food, I decided to confide in her about my struggles with weight.

"How do you do it? How do you stay so thin even after forty!!?"

She told me every single one of her habits. And something clicked.

It's not what she ate that inspired me. No, what got me was that she had figured out how to really nourish herself. With her tastes, her desires, and even her lifestyle. How she wasn't giving up the things she enjoyed, like including the Flore menu in her diet, as she was spending so much time there. How just eating fruits in the morning would allow her a heavier lunch. And also . . .

"Of course, desserts are *juste pas possible*. You forget that the word 'dessert' ever existed."

My first thought was no. That's not possible for me. No, no no no. I have my rules. And my rules, they're ironclad. . . . They're things like:

> Life isn't worth living without a *goûter*. And a *goûter* is defined as a treat you can dunk in your tea.

> Every meal has to finish with something sweet, otherwise it's not a real meal and therefore not real life.

> No self-respecting woman would exercise, because exercise is not cool. Have you ever seen Charlotte Gainsbourg exercising?

And yet when Sophie talked to me about the way she feeds herself, her simplicity and groundedness inspired me.

I took a long hard look at my "rules" and realized that a lot of them were pretty stupid.

I decided to change things.

I started with giving up bread. Not completely, mind you, but remember, I used to be the girl in the restaurant who finished the entire basket of bread before the appetizers arrived. I stopped eating desserts. Not all desserts, mainly cakes and ice cream. I wanted to see what it felt like to end a meal without something sweet.

It's a little tough in the beginning, then you get used to it, and you end up completely forgetting to look at the dessert menu. Right away, I felt positive effects. And not only on my muffin line but also on my self-image. I could eat differently without being totally frustrated. My old "rules" were nothing more than bad habits to hide behind. I finally understood that if I gained some weight, it was my body telling me that it was tired of absorbing my excesses.

Encouraged with my progress, I read books on nutrition and applied some new principles that seemed to work for me. I wasn't following a diet. Or counting calories. I knew I couldn't do that. And I wasn't giving up what I love to eat. I was harmonizing my way of eating with my tastes and my lifestyle and using moderation. And that's really personal. No one else can do that for you, and it would serve no purpose whatsoever if I told you what I was eating. It suits no one but myself.

I started walking again, everywhere, and kept up with a little yoga and Pilates—and I always used the stairs, even though there was an elevator to go up the five floors to my apartment.

And I lost weight.

I'm far from being New York–skinny and that's not at all my goal, but I got back to the weight I knew and the weight where I feel most myself. I accept fluctuations and try to adjust as I go.

Now my friends ask me to be their weight-loss coach. They say that they're inspired by me. . . .

And it just cracks me up.

Seriously? Me? A weight-loss coach? *Non, c'est juste pas possible.* ✗

MY BEAUTY ESSENTIALS

the
brow

Knowing how to style your brows can change your whole face,
giving it more character and style. A simple brow powder will
do, but I also love the Brow Zings eyebrow kit by Benefit.

Danielle Kosann

Brianna Lance

the smoky eye

I found my perfect smoky eye after years of practice.
It takes a while, but once you master the smoky eye,
the rewards are amazing. Now it's my everyday look and
I couldn't go out without it. A smoky eye is magic:
it makes anyone more beautiful and mysterious.

the slicked back hair

This is the remedy for bad hair days and it works at any
length (even for short hair like mine!) All you need is
a good hair gel (I love Kiehl's). It's also great when you
want a look that's special and sophisticated, but your
hairdresser is booked. A lot of us are insecure about giving
our face the spotlight, but we shouldn't be: I've never seen
a woman look anything but elegant with slicked back hair.

THE TURN OF THE SCREW (TURNING 40)

By the time you read these pages, I will be in my forties.
Or dangerously close. Or, if you've picked up the book a little late
(wait, what's your excuse again?), in them completely.

Let me tell you a little bit about how it feels.

Great. Horrible. Shameful. Proud. Old. Young. Ah!!! Nonsense. Yeah. Exactly that.

It's a little bit like teenaging, all over again.

Like the other day, a younger guy flirted with me and I was so shocked that I said to myself: "Are you a pervert, young man?"

That's how stupid you get when you're about to turn forty.

Of course, so many questions surface when age invites itself in. Where am I with my life? Is there still time to make a baby? (I really believed the magazines that said forty was the new thirty. "Your ovaries don't read the same magazines as you do," says my gynecologist.)

Am I happy with my job, my love life? Am I really at the middle of my life? Let me count.

Yes, I am. OH SHIT.

In your head, you're still the same as you were at twenty.

Okay, wiser. Okay, calmer. Okay, less broke. Okay, less attracted to unfitting relationships. Okay, less attracted to crazy nights in dance clubs.

Well, maybe you're not the same. And you like yourself better now, except for a few things.

At forty what hits you is that your body really starts changing. So if you wanted to go about your life and forget that you're getting older, you can't: Your body is there to remind you.

Remember when you hit your teens and your body started to go crazy on you?

Some body parts changed shape and hair grew in weird places?

Same thing. And the same type of insecurity rises from it (damn, just when you thought you had your life together).

Those little shadows under your eyes after a long night of partying?

Now they are deep, dark circles if you stay

up to watch even one extra episode of *Game of Thrones*. They're there even if you haven't watched anything. Actually, the circles are part of you now.

Oh, and that little croissant you liked to reward yourself with once in a while?

Well, now it stays with you (in the form of cellulite on your tummy). Good thing that now you can also probably afford Spanx, 'cause life is nicely made that way.

Those charming "expression wrinkles" you had on your forehead sometimes when you were tired and the lighting was bad?

Well, now they seem to have taken up permanent residence. Oh, and the ones on the sides of your nose? What's up, guys? You too were not invited. Candlelight tonight?

AGE, you party pooper.

Once the physical change is a reality, all of your proudly and loudly voiced opinions ("Fillers make people look crazy!" "Electric-current facials are torture!" "Botox was created for animals!" "All these things are unnatural!" True, false, true, and true) get slightly hushed. And interesting questions start to appear:

"But what if done in moderation?"

"What if I told no one?"

And, most important: "But how old would forty-year-old celebrities look without them?"

Whatever one decides—I have yet to make up my mind about some of these—there are so many ways to cope with aging, from concealer to Pilates to laser to Spanx, that it

would be stupid to spend much time complaining about it.

Which brings me to what I wanted to tell you.

Most of what you hear about getting older is just total made-up forty-year-old bullshit. Don't listen to it.

Because, at forty, I've never felt more free, I've never had more courage, more humor, more success, more fun. Never in my life have I been so good at listening to myself and to others and feeling my life instead of thinking it. Never in my life have I felt so sexy and seductive; never in my life have I been surrounded by such interesting people.

Now that I can talk to you from age forty, I can tell you—don't worry, it's all good. Life is the same, only better. Never perfect, never settled, never figured out, but ever beautifully flowing.

How boring would a figured-out life be anyway?

In my forties (as I tried to do in my twenties), I will live my life as an adventure. Have fun, take care of my body, go see a shrink to answer some of my deep/stupid questions, fail at a good number of things, succeed at a few. Try to love better. Just be me. And laugh at the numbers.

Oh, and I will never call anybody who is attracted to me a pervert. Except if he's running naked after me in the dark. In that case, I'll just turn around and show him my Spanx. That'll do. ✗

ON BEAUTY

ONE ON ONE WITH A WOMAN WHO INSPIRES ME

Drew Barrymore

GD: You have a way of being that is so natural and relaxed. What does beauty mean to you?

DB: (Laughs.) I don't have the DNA to be cool and mysterious. I'm like a Labrador! I think a smile is the best makeup, better than lipstick. And laugh lines are so much cooler than eyeliner. Also, it can't hurt to have a good concealer.

GD: We're both about to turn forty! How do you feel about it? And how should we embrace it?

DB: Whenever I think about the aging process, I immediately cut to an It's a Wonderful Life montage. Without each of my experiences, I wouldn't be who I am today. I believe that I only get better as I get older, so that has to translate to looks too!

GD: You just had a baby, and I love the fact that on some show you basically said, "I wanna take my time losing my baby weight, and fuck the rest."

DB: Yes, I really took my time — like three years! And my husband was the nicest you could ever imagine about it. A woman needs to feel that way when she's going through big, dramatic changes. My feet grew two-and-a-half shoe sizes!

GD: What do you find beautiful in others?

DB: I think beautiful people make the effort and care enough to tell you the truth and to guide you with their words and their time. That's true beauty to me. That, and a good concealer. I really do go back to concealer.

THINGS PARISIANS DO

To the untrained eye, Parisians look a lot like New Yorkers:
Both dress like everyone else in their neighborhood but believe they're totally unique. For Parisians, Paris = France, even if the rest of the country disagrees. (Sound familiar, New Yorkers?) And they are always thinking about how to escape Paris but shed a little tear each time they see the Eiffel Tower.

Aside from those similarities, Parisians and New Yorkers are actually very different.

PARISIANS LOVE . . .

× Complaining, of course. I always forget how much Parisians love to complain. I land in Paris with a sense of sweet joy (Woooooooh, I'm gonna be able to eat a real croissant with real butter in it! And the first one doesn't count.) My adopted New Yorker hysteria lasts till I set foot in a cab.

There is no hello.

Instead, the driver immediately launches into "I'm just warning you, madame, we're gonna get into traffic. And you *really picked the right destination,* eh! (Parisian irony, right there.) Right in the center of the city; what a grreaaat idea. *C'est tout paralysé.* Whaaat? Naaaaaa, I'm not saying you're paralyzed, madame— oh, and she takes offense pretty easily, *la petite madame*! I'm talking about the city! It's the city that's paralyzed! Paris! Oh, but this again, it's because of politicians. You know, the left wing . . ."

Here, beware. You cannot just ignore the cab driver by pretending to have e-mails, like you would in New York.

× What the Parisian loves best is to complain *with* you.

So just know: If a Parisian starts to complain, it is your duty to complain along with him. That's how you make friends in Paris.

× Talking for hours. *Remaking the world,* as we say. The main activity at Parisian dinner parties.

× Going to the Flore, but not sitting on the tourist side—ew. Parisians have their zones, you guys.

× Pretend that you know the waiter and Frédéric Beigbeder (notorious Parisian party animal/writer): "Yeaaah, he's a friend. Yeaaah, he didn't say hello THIS time, but it's a game between us, because we're such good friends, you see?"

× Smoking. Parisians love to smoke. They smoke whenever they can, anywhere you'll let them smoke, and in any weather. They don't mind sitting at a café *terrasse* on a snowy day just so they can smoke. They even still smoke in some clubs. Nobody would dare ask a Parisian to stop smoking.

× Saying "I'm quitting smoking" while lighting a cigarette.

× Driving like a lunatic, parking wherever, being super proud of their Smart car all beaten up by Parisian life, knowing all the shortcuts of Paris.

× Hosting improvised parties. Start drinking an apéro at seven, then hang around, open some wine, and decide to cook an easy (but delicious) pasta while *remaking the world* till four in the morning. Call the neighbors, the single friend who lives three blocks down. Get a little bit tipsy, laugh a lot. Be cool.

× Being frank. The Parisian is nothing if not frank.

"What the hell is that coat?" = It looks so-so on you; we can go back to your place to change it if you want.

× Giving disguised compliments.

"Hey, I haven't received my art print!" = I like your illustrations; congrats on your shop. (I wouldn't say no if you sent me one.)

× Having a family of friends they've known forever, loving and hating them but being ever faithful to them. Spending weekends with them, vacations with them. Not socializing too much outside of that, because who needs more friends? Being ready to do anything for them.

× Being very, very, very careful when a newcomer tries to join the group. Almost cold. Even mean sometimes. For a long time. Maybe a year. Maybe more.

After at least a year or more, saying like it's nothing: "You're coming on vacation with us this summer?" Understanding you've found your family of friends. Being ready to do anything for them. Being very careful with newcomers.

× Shopping at Monop' (a cheap but chic chain store, sort of like the French Target). The Parisian loves Monop', because every French girl grew up close to one. Being able to say, when someone compliments your cashmere sweater: "It's Monop'!" Very Parisian.

× Having very heated conversations. Spending an entire evening arguing on subjects as varied as politics, Kim Kardashian, philosophy, anything, as long as the conversation heats up. Start talking louder. Shouting sometimes. Pretend to be very mad: the definition of a successful Parisian dinner.

× Flirting. Parisians love to flirt. In Paris, here's how it happens:

The Parisian woman:

Pretends she is completely unaware of the guy who's coming on to her, makes fun of him "to test him," ditches him to have drinks with her friends, and makes fun of

TO SAY: "I'M QUITTING SMOKING" WHILE LIGHTING A CIGARETTE.

his DESPERATE texts. Behaves like a real pain in the ass until he falls completely and totally in love with her.

Then maybe she'll agree to give it a try, make him her slave for a year, then decide she loves him and wants to make him a baby. Thinks about getting married, maybe one day, "just for the party."

The Parisian man:

Loves to be super pretentious, thinks he is Serge Gainsbourg, goes out with a dozen girls at the same time, and parties in clubs till dawn. Thinks that all girls are the same, is a total asshole till meeting that pain-in-the-ass girl who has him totally under her thumb, and then becomes the sweetest guy ever.

Makes a baby with her, but forgets to ask her if she'd want to get married.

THINGS PARISIANS SAY:

× "I certainly don't exercise," and actually really not exercising.

× "Today I'm exercising!" Like it was the event of the year. Then trying to go incognito to the gym because you couldn't find any exercise gear except old sweatpants you've been sleeping in since high school.

× "The Marais, it's over!" and then ending up in the Marais. "No, but, Garance, we're talking Haut Marais here! Completely different!"

× *"Merde," "putain," "fait chier"* (like saying "shit" "fuck" "it sucks") every other word, and sometimes all three in a row (when, really, it sucks).

× "Yeah, what can I do? I'm a snob."

× "I should go to the Louvre one of these days. Wanna come with me to the Louvre? Oh, you prefer going to the Bon Marché? All right."

× Talking in negatives.

"It's **not bad**, uh?" = It's good.

"No, but I'm **not** saying I'm **not** liking it" = I like it.

"It's great, **no**?" = It's great, isn't it?

AND PARISIANS HATE . . .

× Waiting in line = The Thing Parisians Hate More than Anything in the World. Parisians hate queuing so much that they've all agreed to hate queuing together. So instead of arranging themselves in a nice line and politely talking and introducing their dogs like in New York, the Parisian will do anything to go first (pretend he's sick, create a double line, a triple line, pretend he knows someone at the front of the line), and it creates a general mess where everyone ends up pushing and insulting one another.

× Crossing at the green light. It's much better to throw yourself under a car than to wait.

× The Parisian woman hates taking the subway, but she sort of has to, because of the *trafic de merde*. And because she's a smart one, she has developed the Dr. Jekyll and Mr. Hyde–subway technique:

She walks down the street, fast, chic, full of allure.

She steps into the subway and suddenly transforms—maybe it's the way she folds her scarf to hide half her face, or the way she takes her hat down, puts her shoulders up, and the expression "don't talk to me or I'll kill you!!!" Anything to ensure that no one will notice her or talk to her, because, really, the subway is a pain, "even more on my line, Garance, I swear, my line really sucks."

And then she emerges from the subway, puts everything back in place, stands straight, walks fast, chic, with allure. Chic, yes, but not in the metro.

× Working during vacation. (Which is healthy, no?)

Don't you ever, ever, ever try to contact a Parisian during vacation. Not only will you find a saturated voice mail, but your number will be forever blocked from that Parisian's phone.

Calling during vacations? WHO DOES THAT???

× Other drivers: Honk, shout, and use body language. A raised hand, completely folded except for the middle finger, expresses frustration over not being the only car driving around the Arc de Triomphe.

× Other bikers: No pity for those stupid people who go super slow on the bike lane with their broken bikes (yep, choosing a perfectly functioning bike is an art that one has to learn). Right to insult = *oui*.

× Other pedestrians: Let out a very loud sigh and power walk to get in front of a slow walker, when a simple "excuse me" could have worked just as well.

× Tourists, even when the Parisian himself is a tourist. Hating other tourists when you're in Paris—all right, we get it.

But hating tourists when you're in New York and yourself a tourist, that is very, very Parisian. ✕

Yves Saint La
said it first, a
"Sans élégance
il n'y a pas d'e

urent
d best,
e cœur,"
égance.

Caroline Issa

Élégance de Cœur

Yves Saint Laurent said it first, and best,
"Sans élégance de cœur, il n'y a pas d'élégance."

As much as I love fashion, I agree that true elegance is found elsewhere.

It's in the way we behave with others.

Some call it manners, or etiquette, but to me it's deeper than that, because good manners are just a matter of culture. Did you know that opening a present in front of the person who gave it to you is considered very rude in Japan? You're supposed to take it home and open it privately.

Whereas in France, not opening it right away would be like saying, "I couldn't care less about your present!"

I've tried many times to fit into the cultures of the different places where I've been, but after a few major fails I've decided to rely on what my heart tells me.

In France, we call that *"élégance de cœur,"* elegance of heart. I know, it sounds cheesy.

But you know what? True elegance is also knowing when one should be cheesy.

Let me tell you how I discovered *élégance de cœur. . . .*

You could probably say I'm at ease with myself.

I've even made it my profession. I talk about myself every day on my blog.

It's ironic, because I used to be desperately shy.

I remember turning bright red anytime I had to say something in front of a group.

As a kid, it made my life very difficult at school. Asking to go to the bathroom was torture, so I just didn't do it. I would suffer a whole day. Answering a teacher's question out loud was impossible for me. I would melt in front of the class and feel terrible for weeks, telling my mom I never wanted to go to school ever again.

To make up for never talking in public, I was a very applied and sweet pupil.

I had very few friends; I felt different and a bit awkward.

It got a little bit better when I became a teenager. The shy kid turned into a deep, passionate teenager. A very INTENSE (dramatic voice inflection) teenager. I had a very close circle of friends. Two friends, to be exact. Two of the nerdiest girls at school.

We would have philosophical conversations, smoke cigarettes, drink coffee, and feel pretty special.

Then one day, when I was about fifteen, Anne happened.

Anne was my exact opposite. Blond, loud, fun, easy. Total tomboy, complete lightness of being; imagine Cameron Diaz with a French accent. She was always laughing at herself, making fun of her mistakes, and she had a sunny confidence that drew people to her.

She was the daughter of diplomats, so she had traveled the world, lived everywhere, spoke four languages, had met presidents and hung out with paupers, and she would talk with the same passion about both.

I was fascinated. We fell into the most passionate friendship, and my world suddenly opened.

She made me laugh. She laughed at me. "Why are you so serious?" she said. Having grown up with two big brothers, she was outspoken; she would stand up for herself, fight if necessary.

She also didn't have much of an ego.

But what she radiated was not only self-assurance—it was simpler than that: She didn't think anyone was above or beneath her.

She would talk with a teacher with the same candor she would use with a friend. She would treat everyone equally and expect the same for herself. She just was who she was

and instinctively knew that was the only way she could be.

This was probably the lesson of my life.

In her presence, I relaxed. I understood how my fears, my shyness, my bright redness, were actually a lot about how self-conscious I was, worried about myself and what people would think of me before considering the person I was connecting with.

I let that go, little by little. I got really interested in how other people were feeling, in what they were saying, what they were expressing with their body language. How could I make them feel at ease with me?

I learned to laugh at myself. At my quirks, my shyness. I would say something like, "Am I turning bright red right now? Because I can feel my cheeks burning."

It would throw people off, make them laugh, change the energy in the conversation.

It would draw them closer, because it was human, honest, and simple.

I dared to ask questions. Like Anne, I decided that there was no shame in not knowing something. Instead of making situations more complicated by pretending, I would simply say, "I have no idea what you're talking about. . . ." And people would explain. They would actually love to explain.

I got the memo. The world wasn't going to stop if I made a mistake or said something stupid.

I was not that important, I realized. Other people go through the same emotions— feel awkward, don't know what to say, don't know how to act. Just admitting it breaks the spell and creates ease and comfort.

As I got good at laughing at myself, I experienced the joy of making other people laugh, just by being my very imperfect self.

And I discovered the joy of connecting, which to this day defines everything I am.

I don't know if Anne ever realized the gift she gave me.

But today I hope I can do the same thing for others. If I make people feel good, if I encourage them to be themselves and be at ease, then I feel happy and present.

To me, that's the heart of elegance. ✕

I LEARNED TO LAUGH AT MYSELF

How to not fuck up your hello

Hello is the most important word of your day.

Do you know how I can tell if we're going to have a good day at the studio? How well things are going with the team? It's in the way we all say hello to each other in the morning.

Saying hello takes less than a second. It's the easiest thing in the world to do, yet so many people completely miss the opportunity. It's too bad, because with a beautiful hello you can change the atmosphere in a room— it acknowledges the people around you; it makes them feel present and important (they are).

French as I am, I go totally Italian on this one.

I love a clear, genuine, warm hello.

You have one shot at hello with each person you see during your day. Don't fuck it up! Use your hello for good. For a lesson in what not to do, here are three examples of . . .

WAYS TO FUCK UP YOUR HELLO

THE HALFWAY HELLO

This one is subtle, but subtlety is of the essence in interpersonal relationships.

The halfway hello. Aaaaah, you were almost there; why did you let it get away?

It's entering a room and throwing your hello in the air like you just don't care, without looking at people.

It's saying hello to someone while at the same time looking over their shoulder to see if there is someone else more important in the room, or looking to the side to see what's on TV, or looking down to see their shoes (only allowed if followed by "Oh my God, sorry, I got distracted. I love your shoes so much!").

It's saying hello with a strange expression, leaving the recipient of your hello worried for the rest of the day. (Was she sick? Was she mad at me? Is she having an affair with my husband? Did she just get Botox?)

THE SLACKER HELLO

I once hired a young woman who, every morning, would show up at the office with a giant venti double-shot iced caramel macchiato in her hands and an expression that meant either:

1. She'd had very bad sex last night— not a good look.

2. This was the very very very last venti double-shot iced caramel macchiato she would ever hug against her chest, because Starbucks was banning her from the store forever.

3. Her puppy had just died. Or something equally bad.

Her hello was an exhausted whisper, accompanied by eyes rolled up to the sky. I'm sure she wanted this to come across as something like "I am so important, yet my life is so filled with drama. What wonder will I accomplish today?" But it came off more as "I'm so bored already and it's only nine o'clock. What unimportant task will I have to slack off through today?"

These entrances gave everyone in the office micro-anxiety attacks for a while, then we all had to start laughing about it (and, I'm sorry to report, imitating her behind her back), and then one day we decided it was time to part ways. Pheeeew.

THE ASSHOLE HELLO

In fashion, the beautiful hello is an art that most powerful people have mastered. It's often at the lower levels—though still high enough to inflate a weak ego—that the disease strikes.

But positions change very fast in fashion. People remember. The intern remembers. You can fuck up your hello once (it happens, even to the best), but don't do it twice.

I'm sure it's the same at your school or in your business. That's the way it works, so here are the basics:

If you've met someone and have been properly introduced, you should say hello the next time you see them. The simplest of hellos will do. Pretending not to see them either means that you're blind and not wearing glasses (meaning you're old and vain) or that you're simply an asshole.

If you're sitting next to someone at a dinner, you should say hello and introduce yourself.

You should also try to exchange a few words.

You could also not introduce yourself and turn your back to talk to the person on your other side for the whole dinner. But that would mean you're an asshole.

If, say, you're speaking to Beyoncé and your doorman passes by (I know, but weird situations do happen), say hello to your doorman—nothing fancy, just a nice nod. He will understand that you are presently talking with a very important person.

There's nothing worse than changing the way you address someone depending on the situation you're in. Hello is a set currency between two people.

Even if you really wish you'd never been introduced to someone, unless they've hurt you very badly and it's war, say hello. That's the way society works; we're not animals. Anything less would be rude.

Remember, hello is such a wonderful opportunity! Use all these free hellos to send good vibes out into the world, to build your persona, and as an opportunity to smile more.

We all look better when we're smiling anyway. ✗

WE ALL LOOK BETTER WHEN WE'RE SMILING ANYWAY.

XO

the

thank-you note

A COMPETITIVE SPORT

In my world, the thank-you note is a *pretty important thing*.

It's kind of expected.

Feared, almost.

You say thank you all the time. Thank you for a present, of course. Thank you for dinner, obviously. Thank you for giving me that job. Thank you for working for me. Thank you for interviewing me. Thank you for letting me interview you.

Thank you, thank you, thank you.

Thank you for thanking me too. Yep, like Russian dolls. Just imagine:

Somebody sends you flowers to say thank you for a beautiful collaboration.

You should thank that person for the thank-you flowers.

And you might—I mean IT'S NOT IMPOSSIBLE, but you might receive a thank-you note thanking you for your thank-you note. I swear.

At the very least you might get a thank-you e-mail.

The last one standing wins? That's the way it plays in New York.

I am not sure about thank-you-note practices in Paris, but I don't remember being thanked that much. Not at all, actually.

I don't know if that's because at the time I was living there the things I was doing were not worth thanking or if it's because Paris is more of a thankless city.

But in any case, back then I was not thanking around as much myself.

When I got to New York, people must have thought I was very impolite to not thank officially. Brrrrr, dark, dark days for la Doré.

I ENDED UP LEARNING IT BY LIVING IT, AND TODAY I'M SHARING MY THANK-YOU-NOTE SCIENCE WITH YOU. HERE IT IS:

× A thank-you note can be almost anything, as long as it comes from the heart.

× It can be a doodle made on a napkin with a Bic pen, and you can keep it pretty informal. Or it can be a beautiful personalized note on proper stationery, written with a delicate fountain pen ("Thank you for this enchanting dinner . . .").

Dearest Garance,

I think you are in Miami, sick as a dog and I hope that by the time you get this note you are feeling _much_ better — always happens when you start to unwind. grrr...

Anyhow ! A big thank you for the lunches you fed us at - I can see from all the amazing comments for the videos that they were a _huge_, _huge_ success — as we knew they would be ☺

Chère Garance, ... t'écris ce mot à la main ... loved our tweet ... mercí. Olivier

olivier theyskens

MERCI BEAUCOUP

ALSO, DON'T FORGET:

× It should feel personal. Include an intimate detail or a short anecdote.

× Keep it simple. Handwriting is enough to express how much you care.

× A thank-you note can be late if you apologize with a sense of humor. But if you don't know how much of a sense of humor your recipient has, send on the earlier side.

× End with a simple closing. "Love," "Best," "With Love," depending on the person.

× Write the address in your own hand.

That's it! As simple as that.

I'm sorry to report, though, that to this day I am not really sure about when to stop the Russian-dolls thank-you effect. So I just thank everybody, all the time.

Thank you for reading this.

No, thank you.

No, I insist, thank _you_! ×

Chère Garance,
Quel bonheur de
t'avoir avec nous
au dîner Carven...
Merci !!!
Fais moi signe
quand tu es à
Paris... s'il te pl
Je t'embras

CARVEN
collection femme été 2

Guillaume

Firenze Marzo 2011

Garance,
"... picture y our ou your
c'est Magnifique !!!
MASSIMILIANO GIORNETTI
"We forward
mia vo

garance

André*

Thank you for your collaboration
and your time. I hope you like
the magazine.

Hope to see you soon.

love

Dear Garance,

I loved meeting you in
New York! Hope to see you in
Paris ... Stay cool gal!
x Stella

E-MAIL MADE ME

A BAD PERSON

If e-mail didn't exist, you'd say I was
a pretty adorable woman with a French accent.

But e-mail does exist. I still don't understand how it all went down. One day, somebody decided, "E-mail is the modern way to communicate!!!" and, just like that, it took over our lives.

It's true that in the meantime I decided to start a blog.

You can't have a blog and not do e-mail.

Yes. I thought for a moment I could be like Ralph Lauren and not do e-mail.

But I'm not Ralph Lauren. My level of coolness doesn't negate my need to answer e-mail. So beware, Ralph. I'm working on it.

I'm me, and if you send me an e-mail, I swear I will desperately try to answer you.

But I might not succeed. Here are the reasons why. Try not to hate me, okay?

FIRST, YOU NEED TO KNOW, I CAN'T TYPE.

I type slowly. I type with two fingers only, and I envy you terribly, all of you who can use all ten fingers to type. But I can think of a million things I'd rather do than spend time in front of my screen to learn how to type.

And you're right, it's completely counterproductive for a writer to spend half her day pecking away with two fingers. I have to work on it. Till I do, e-mailing takes time and way too much finger power.

THEN THERE IS THE UNSTOPPABLE E-MAIL FLOW.

FROM MY TEAM AND MY AGENTS

I answer these e-mails most times, because they're always urgent and important, and also because I know I can answer in "Garance," a special language that only people who know me well can understand.

It goes something like this:

"Yts I'll be there abut <i can't go to ealry. Dont expet me bfore 930 I have a thing before zsxxxxxG love you"

I know. It's absolutely rude to expect people to decipher my e-mail language. Only bad, rude people do that.

I TOLD YOU.

FROM CLIENTS OR POTENTIAL CLIENTS

× After five minutes in my in-box: Ah, this is important. I can't just answer on the fly in "Garance." I'm going to flag this and respond when I have space and time to formulate the perfect answer.

× After one day in my in-box: Oh noooo! That flagged e-mail! I forgot about it! I have to answer it as soon as I am back at the studio. It's so important! I am going to resend it to myself. And set a reminder. If I let two days pass I will definitely lose that job.

× After three days (and three flags and ten alerts): OH MY GAAAWD, the e-maaaail!!! I must stop everything I'm doing and answer right away. It's okay if it's short and "sent from my iPhone," right? No? Well, what choice do I have, REALLY!?!

A late, rushed e-mail to a client from your iPhone? That looks bad.

Rude!!! And worse: unprofessional. (The worst insult you can give anybody in America. If you want to see people turn red and give you bad service forever, just try it)

I TOLD YOU.

I know what you're thinking: Why not just set aside a time to answer e-mail?

Because I've tried. It ends up eating 80 percent of my morning. It drives me crazy.

FROM MY FAMILY AND FRIENDS

Unless I receive it right at the moment when I am bored AND online, I tell myself that I'll answer as soon as I have the time to write a nice, fun response with news in it, and jokes, and photos, and questions, and everything a great e-mail should be.

So I put it aside for later, when I'll have time, which is NEVER.

It's bad because not only does my family hate that I never respond to e-mail, they also worry about me. Then they follow up with a text: "We're worried. Are you okay?"

Letting the people you love worry about you is so, so, so bad. So rude. Only bad people do that.

I TOLD YOU.

I finally decided that I had to address the e-mail disaster that was becoming my life (losing jobs, breaking up with friends, my family disowning me), and I hired an assistant.

My assistant is diligent, always answers on time, with real words and no smileys (I use a lot of smileys, which is immature AND unprofessional), and it solved a lot of my problems.

When I need to respond to someone directly, she's on my back till I want to kill her. And she handles—very professionally—anything that I don't need to respond to myself.

She also answers anybody who is nice enough to understand that I have a problem with e-mail and who won't be shocked that I don't answer personally.

Sometimes she even e-mails with my friends to set up a night out. Or deals with my family, planning a vacation in Morocco, because otherwise there would be no vacation in Morocco with my family.

It's okay, it sort of works. But I know deep down how rude it is. SO rude. Absolutely rude.

Also, one day my assistant might tell me she's going to Morocco with my family in my place.

She would be right to do so. I deserve it. I'm a bad person. All because of e-mail. ✕

YTS I'LL BE THERE ABUT <I CAN'T GO TO EALRY. DONT EXPET ME BFORE 930 I HAVE A THING BEFORE ZSXXXXG LOVE YOU

Netiquette

EXCITING
FESTIVE
ONE·OF·A·KIND
MEMORABLE
VIVACIOUS
CAREFREE
HAPPY
BIRTHDAY!

How *crazy* do we get with our phones?

We risk collision with a car/person/pole every two minutes because we can't resist texting while walking.

We spend a fortune on our data plans, instead of on that beautiful pair of shoes we've just Instagrammed (yes, I'm talking about you, international data roaming), and we broadcast things to the world that we'd never want our moms to stumble on (yes, your mom *is* following you).

I guess we need some ground rules, and our rules need to change as we go, because, as you know, the minute you've mastered one form of social media, a new one pops up with a vengeance, more fun, more cool, more demanding of your time, and triggering a whole new set of social anxieties.

So, in order to try to stay cool and, hmm, *socially aware,* let's develop some social-media etiquette and beware of . . .

THINGS THAT MAKE PEOPLE NEVER CALL US AGAIN

× Checking your phone on a date, in a business meeting, at a job interview, dinner, or wedding. Basically, taking your phone out during any interaction when you should be focused on the people present—sex included—is wrong.

NB: Checking your phone under the table is neither discreet nor respectful. It makes people believe that you can't meet their eyes because you think they are stupid. They won't understand that you're looking at your phone under the table.

Or, worse, they will just think that you are staring at your crotch while they're speaking.

That person will never have dinner with you again.

THINGS THAT MAKE PEOPLE HATE US

× Laughing out loud while checking your phone at the office. It makes everyone else feel like you're laughing at them (and that you're not working). If you let it happen one day and it is an exception, share the joke.

× Talking on your phone on the bus. Sending texts during a movie. Having a crazy *Jaws* ringtone. Reading Twitter jokes out loud (oops, I do that all the time). Listening to very, very loud music with your earphones and thinking nobody else can hear it.

THINGS THAT MAKE US LOOK VERY STUPID

×   Taking your phone to the bathroom in a restaurant. It will eventually fall in the water and then you'll have to ask the waiter to bring you a glass of uncooked rice to put your phone in. (Yes, it sucks up the humidity. You didn't get that from me.)

×   Taking secret pictures of people. When you do, that's always when the flash decides to pop, and I'm not saying that because I tried to sneak a photo at AntiGravity yoga and got blinded by my own flash in front of the whole class.

THINGS THAT MAKE US LOOK LIKE WE HAVE NO SELF-AWARENESS

×   "Spotted: I think I just saw @VictoriaBeckham at my nail spa on 45th and 5th!"

I mean, for starters, it's a little #WhoGivesaShit about where Victoria Beckham is—Okay, to be honest, it's our natural instinct to be a bit voyeuristic.

But it's not okay to share other people's lives without asking them. This is not sharing; this is papara-gramming. And it's wrong.

×   "Me and my boo at Starbucks this morning. He has a latte and I do blonde roast. Both venti. Isn't that love?"

Please, don't be that couple. Be your own person.

However you try to spin it, sharing your love for your boyfriend, your baby, your dad, your mom, should be restricted to twice a year. I know, it's hard. But I really, really don't care about your mom. Really I don't. Unless she's Victoria Beckham, obviously.

×   "Look, my baby just threw up on my Balenciaga shirt!!! OMG, how cute!!! #mybabychloe #baby #love #happiness."

I'm more tolerant of babies just because I know parents literally can't help it. It's like a monster has taken them over. They're not themselves. It takes two years, or forever. Hang tight; be a good friend.

×   "Me and my friend @garancedore OMGOMGOMG, totally wasted!!!"

Tagging people without asking permission first is really, really bad. Not funny. Anything implying that you're in a state of wastedness should stay private anyway. Also, Garance, I know her—she never gets wasted.

"Follow me!!!"

If you're under fifteen, it's totally cute. If you're over fifteen, it's totally desperate.

OKAY, SORRY, JUST RECEIVED A TEXT, GOTTA GO. ×

"FOLLOW ME!!!"

IF YOU'RE UNDER 15, IT'S TOTALLY CUTE.

IF YOU'RE OVER 15,

IT'S TOTALLY DESPERATE.

ELEGANCE IS NOT . . .

I like to make fun of myself,
so of course I am pretty quick to make fun of others, too.
But I try as much as I can to not judge.

Because usually when I make a snap judgment about someone, I realize later that I was wrong.

As we've seen, not everybody follows the same etiquette. From Paris to London to New York to Tokyo, the rules are different.

Plus, everyone acts like an asshole, has disastrous style (some make it a signature!), or cuts the line at Starbucks once in a while. What? You've never done it?

Okay, so you get it. I am all for love and compassion. Still, there are a few times where I can't help but judge.

DRESSING IN STATEMENT CLOTHES FROM HEAD TO TOE

Statement on statement on statement: wrong statement.

It's a very soft judgment, but what I see is insecurity.

I know it's not hurting anybody to be a walking advertisement—if it makes the person

happy, why not? But to judge someone as insecure is still to judge.

DANCING HALF-NAKED IN FRONT OF A BUNCH OF GUYS

As a woman, when I see another woman in this situation it saddens me and the big sister in me comes out. I want to go throw a robe over her, but she would be the first one to tell me I'm crazy. I really do believe that we are all sisters and that we should watch out for one another.

It's not an extra-bad judgment. It's kind of funny from a distance. But deep down, it hurts to watch.

I try to send telepathic messages: "You don't need to do that to be loved!!! Be careful!!! They're taking pictures!" But she doesn't give a damn about what I think, because, as we all do, she'll learn on her own.

That said, if you happen to be my friend, it's not gonna be telepathic and it's not a robe I would throw on you; it's a whole ice bucket.

EVERYONE DESERVES RESPECT AND A "HELLO, HOW ARE YOU?"

BEING THE GIRL WHO DOESN'T EAT

I know I shouldn't judge, because it's a deep and very difficult problem, but a girl who doesn't eat 'cause "she's so not hungry!", who orders a tea in lieu of a lunch and takes out a Ziploc with three undefined grains for dessert, makes me want to run to the other side of the world, like, to Brooklyn, let's say.

I don't want to address it, and I don't want to pretend I haven't noticed. I've tried both, and it's just impossible. It's not my role. I can't be a silent witness, but I also can't help. I am sorry. I judge, and I flee.

TALKING DOWN TO MY TEAM

Once again, we're all guilty once in a while of being an ass, being in a rush, being too brusque.

But I don't understand people who talk down to those who work with me.

There, I judge.

Why is it okay to talk down to someone who's "below you"? Do you think I'll never find out? Don't you know my assistant might be your boss one day (she's sort of already mine)? And that even if that never happens, everyone deserves respect and a "hello, how are you?"

I just don't get it; it drives me crazy.

EXTREME GOSSIP

Believe me, I LOVE a good bit of gossip, and if we were at the café, you and I, I would give you a few that would make you laugh out loud.

But there are boundaries. Seriously. I call that "disgusting gossip." Disgossip?

Health problems that people don't want to share, who's having sex with whom, or any other intel way too private to be brought up in the social scene.

That kind of gossip is a real violation, in my book.

When someone I don't know well gives me that type of gossip, I freak out. I don't know what to do with it, I don't want to know, I want to bury my face in the sand, forget what I heard, and try to never see the offender again.

That's about it! Those are my deal-breakers. For the rest, do whatever you will. I'm all love and compassion! ✗

Elegance is ...

× A sincere smile. Not necessarily a perfect smile, but a radiant one.

× A taxi driver waiting for you to get through your front door to make sure you are safe. Rare but beautiful.

× Having a great sense of humor, and being able to laugh at yourself. Works even better if you're George Clooney or Barack Obama.

× Attention to others. Have you ever met someone who, when they look into your eyes, makes you feel like the most interesting person in the world?

× Bringing fresh flowers for no reason.

× Politeness. It can seem unnecessary, I know, but wherever you are, knowing a few basic rules of politeness and being able to apply them naturally, without being obvious, is so elegant.

× Holding the door. Please, hold the door. I'm sorry—I know it's old school, but it's so worth it.

× Quitting in an honorable way. Tipping in a generous way. Winning in a flamboyant way: Being chic doesn't mean being self-effacing.

× Knowing when to make an entrance (too early is before your host has finished cooking their turkey, and too late is once the turkey is cold), and knowing how to make an exit—not the first, not the last, right in the middle.

× Reacting to the small accidents of life with laughter.

× A sense of culture that isn't flaunted or in your face but one that just shows that you are open to the world! Culture is the chicest accessory in the world. Read a book.

× Apologizing. Sincerely. Explaining why you were wrong, to show that you really took the time to think about it. Giving someone time to come back to you. Understanding if they never do.

× Being able to say no without explaining but in a manner that will make people respect it.

× Eloquence. Knowing how to speak. (The secret? Reading and practicing.)

× A waiter running after you to give you your phone back.

× Kindness. I love people who are kind. To me, kindness is the trait of kings. Kind people who don't profer hasty judgments are often the most intelligent ones.

× Someone who asks, kindly, what seat number you're sitting in. And laughs with you when you realize you've made a mistake with your seat.

× A friend waiting with you till you get your cab.

× Giving back. To a charity, to the young, or to the old. Sharing what you've learned, passing it on.

× Giving the people you love freedom, compassion, and understanding.

× Giving yourself freedom, compassion, and understanding. That's very elegant. ✕

ON ELEGANCE

ONE ON ONE WITH A WOMAN WHO INSPIRES ME

Jenna Lyons

GD: What does elegance mean to you?

JL: To me, elegance is someone who can apologize. I know that may not sound like your typical idea of elegance, but it's so important.

GD: What's your policy on thank-you notes?

JL: I never send a thank-you note for a proper gift over e-mail. The exception is if someone sends me flowers or something that's perishable. Otherwise, take five minutes, pull out your stationery, and write a proper thank-you note.

GD: I once saw on your wall: "Thank you for the meatloaf sandwich, love." Was that a thank-you note?

JL: Yes! That's from Tom Sachs. He came in and we had lunch, and afterward he just used a Sharpie and some white paper. But I love that. It didn't take him much time, but it felt meaningful.

GD: How do you manage social media and the selfie trend?

JL: I'm six foot three in heels, so everyone is shorter than me. When the selfie thing first started, people would ask, "Can I take a picture with you?" and I would agree, but then they were always taking the picture up my nose. I had to do something! Today I have one requirement: I get to take the picture.

GD: You are known for changing the rules for elegant evening wear, which I think is amazing. How do you do it?

JL: Over time I've found I feel most elegant when I'm being myself. For me, that means wearing a men's cashmere sweater with a feather skirt. But I wouldn't expect everyone to break the rules if they're not comfortable with it. Doing what's right for you is where you are going to be your most elegant.

GD: What's the secret to elegance at work?

JL: I work with talented people who are constantly putting their hearts on the page. When you do work like this, there are no right answers. So when I give feedback, I always try to find a way to positively reinforce someone's work, even if I am telling them no.

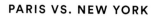

PARIS VS. NEW YORK

PERFECTION

In New York, the city of perfection,
you have the constant feeling of being a little bit out of it:
like, you're doing okay, but you could always do better.

No big deal, as long as you decide that being perfect is not your goal in life. But you'd almost have to make yourself a T-shirt that says I DON'T CARE ABOUT PERFECT (or FUCK PERFECT, if you're Cara Delevingne) to get people to leave you in peace with your averageness.

Because here, and, in fashion in particular, the cult of perfection is really tough, even though we all love *Girls*! (It's so nice to see normal people on TV!!!)

And today, after almost five years of carrying out sociological studies in New York, it seems to me that the pursuit of perfection has its roots in the search for . . .

THE PERFECT MAN.

And looking for him in New York is a serious thing. So. Serious. Too serious.

You'd better not mess up. We're going to get into how that can happen. But first, so that you understand where I'm coming from, let me explain how this goes in France.

Oh, don't worry. It's going to be quick.

For us French people—you meet someone.

It might be a friend you've had for a long time or someone you've just met in a bar. Suddenly it clicks. You talk for hours. You kiss. You might sleep together right away, if you want to. Anyway, you don't make a big deal of it.

The next day, if the guy (or the girl) is still there and you've made them a coffee, BOOM. It's done.

You're boyfriend and girlfriend! Woooh, as simple as that.

And no need to go looking elsewhere: You don't try out the merchandise in France.

You like someone, and you go for it, right away.

If it doesn't work out, then a bit later you have a nice heartbreak, which gives you the occasion to smoke cigarettes while sitting at a café on a rainy day—a very cinematic outcome, indeed.

Maybe that's where we get our super-romantic reputation. We don't shy away from love.

And maybe that's why people are so fascinated by our lack of concern for perfection? Who knows.

In the States, you date. What's a date? A "date" is a guy you "see." It means you plan evenings or days together, you learn about each other. It may mean that you kiss, or not. You may sleep with the guy the first night, or not until weeks later.

But dating doesn't mean you are "with" him. You're not his girlfriend; he's not your boyfriend. He's just a guy you're dating, and it's perfectly possible that he's dating other girls too. And you totally have the right to date other guys; he wouldn't have anything to say about it.

When I make big eyes at people as they tell me this, they always say, "But it makes sense!!! How else would you know which person is the best for you?"

It's like some kind of extreme casting call—*Survivor* style (the last person left standing on a buoy in the middle of an ocean of failed love stories wins). It's a type of natural selection where everything about the guy is a test—from the places he likes to eat ("He took me to eat a BURGER! Can you imagine? MEAT? I'll NEVER reply to his texts again, do you hear me?") to all his different skills (sexual, professional, does he wear a pair of Common Projects like he should?), and you can test him to your heart's content without actually having to commit to a relationship, until you feel he could be a real candidate for being your future husband.

Marriage is such an institution in the States. It's basically the sign that a person "Wins at Life."

I won't even get into how weddings are the culmination of years of fantasizing and social pressure (as you can see in the million romantic comedies about weddings that always end well). Let's just focus on the myth of the perfect man.

SO, WHO IS THE PERFECT MAN?

Well, you can't trust American movies where the woman (who is adorable, beautiful, stylish, funny, and has a good job) ends up with the nerd (who is slightly chubby, not fully employed, and a little awkward, but so funny and irresistible!!!). These movies were written by the nerdy guys.

That's not how it works in real life—sorry, I mean in New York.

In New York, to be perfect, a guy has to have a really great job (first criteria), has to be attractive (but mainly just the great job—stable, well paid, respectable), has to be relatively not too much of a jerk, and . . . well, that's about it, actually.

Pffff, it's easy to be the perfect man in New York.

What's not so easy is being the perfect woman. There's a big imbalance. Because there are loads of amazing women in New York, apparently like five times more than there are guys.

So let's take a look at our perfect woman. And pardon my clichés, okay?

THE PERFECT NEW YORK WOMAN HAS THE PERFECT NEW YORK BODY.

So you got the memo: New York girls are thin and muscular, and anyone who doesn't have that "perfect" body is seen as the nice friend who isn't really in the game (I happen to think those are the girls who are really winning at life, but, once again, that's just my personal point of view as a girl who's a little off in her own world).

I don't have any proof that this is actually what the New York guy is looking for, but I'm going to assume based on what I've seen.

Just think for a second about all the hours we spend at the gym. You have to work to be perfect. On top of already having, well, a real job.

THE PERFECT NEW YORK WOMAN HAS THE PERFECT NEW YORK JOB.

And that's no easy task.

I was talking to a friend who works in PR (a great job, when you think about it. You can get into all the cool parties!), and she was telling me that the guy she was dating was dating another girl at the same time (I warned you!). This other girl had a dream job in travel (so much better than getting into cool parties— you can fly off on cool trips for free!).

The real problem was that this guy was also dating (I know what you're thinking, and I have no idea what the limit is on how many people you can date at once) a model.

That pretty much tops it all, even if the only real benefit to dating a model is being able to say, "My girlfriend is a model."

Aw, yeah, but give the guy a break; it must feel pretty good.

And having that dream job, in the city of dreams, it's not easy.

So it's the battle of the dream jobs. Maybe what you really want is a job where you can sit at your computer all day procrastinating, a job that doesn't stress you out. But I'm sorry to report: That doesn't look so good on a date.

THE PERFECT NEW YORK WOMAN HAS A SET OF PERFECTLY EDITED FRIENDS.

She has her BFF, of course, whom she has known since kindergarten. Then there is the BFF of the moment, the one she wants to be seen with at parties. (Okay, now I'm being cynical. But this whole story is cynical, so don't pretend it bothers you. Plus, I'm French, and cynicism is our religion! I tricked you with that super-romantic illustration, didn't I?)

Then she has her lawyer friends and her friends in finance, for the day when she needs investors (and apparently they're also good contacts for finding a husband). She also has her group of happy artist friends who like to party (nice but a little loud), her powerful friends (CEOs, EICs), her famous friend (if you live in New York and you don't know anyone at least a little bit famous, you don't live in New York).

And, of course, her gay friend; how could I forget? She calls him her gay husband.

Such a network takes years to create, but you must persevere! Perseverance is a sign that you're a perfect girl who never gives up.

AND THAT WAS JUST THE BASICS.

Like the ABCs of perfection.

ADD TO THAT A FEW MORE SELECTIONS FROM THE MENU.

In order of importance:

1. Have a great apartment. Okay, it depends on your age, but a great apartment counts. It has to have a doorman (who knows why, but having a doorman is a sign of social success in New York. I don't have a doorman, so I guess I'm screwed) or—even better— a rooftop!

2. In the right neighborhood. If the apartment in question is in Harlem (even if we all agree that Harlem is THE up-and-coming neighborhood), it's not as good as if it's in the West Village; just know that.

3. Have amazing clothes! Yep, in New York, you'd better have fashion connections. So you can wear all the clothes you can't afford to buy yourself, like Carrie Bradshaw did. (Now I finally understand how she got all those amazing clothes on a journalist's salary! She had friends in PR!)

4. Be "in the know." Know all the good restaurants. Know the owner of the restaurant so you can snag a table at the last minute. Get into a club in the blink of an eye. A huge plus, you have to admit.

Yeah.

It's a lot.

Of things to do.

And you can't just do them. You have to do them perfectly, if possible.

AND YOU HAVE TO MAKE IT LOOK TOTALLY NATURAL.

That, my friends, is the pièce de résistance, and it's what causes the most chaos in my little French brain. You have to do all of this and, on top of it all, act like you're cool about it all.

You can't be good at everything in a city as stressful as New York AND be relaxed about it. To reach that degree of perfection, there's some part of you that has to be a control freak. But since no one likes a control freak, you find yourself saying things like:

"I love burgers!!! They're my favorite thing!"

"I'm such a party girl!!!"

"I love beer!"

"This apartment? Nah, I decorated it myself little by little, with my best friend" (best friend = my decorator).

"I'm real, you know, friendship is a deep thing for me."

So there you have it. It took me almost five years to decode, but now I've finally understood—nobody perfect is cool, and nobody cool is perfect. ✗

NOBODY

PERFECT

IS COOL,

AND NOBODY

COOL IS

PERFECT.

With love, *we're*
stumbling and
as life unfolds. A
why, *whatever ha*
we must *keep ou*

ids forever,

arning

nd this is

pens,

hearts open.

the L word

One day I was on the phone with my father,
whom I don't call nearly enough, and I was trying to communicate just how much I love him.

"Papa, I love you!"

Silence.

"Uhhhhh, Papa?"

"Yes, my dear?"

"I love you!"

"I'm sorry. I didn't hear you. What did you say?"

"Ummm. Okay . . . I miss you!"

"Yeahhhh, yeah yeah yeah. You too, my dear. I miss you a lot."

No, my father and I aren't having relationship issues. We love each other! It's just that in France you don't throw around "I love you" casually. My father misheard me because "I love you" (how American of me) just didn't register. In France, "I love you" is strong. "I love you" is dramatic. "I love you" runs deep.

Of course, there are degrees. Some families never say it (which isn't to say they don't love each other), and some families, like mine, only say it at special moments. Some say it often too, but in my experience those families are rare.

Imagine my surprise when, a year after I moved to the States, I got an e-mail from an American friend who ended her note with "I love you!"

Wait, what? I spent a half hour reading and rereading the e-mail.

"I love you." Wait, you "loooooooove" me? How exactly do you mean? Do you mean like LOVE love? Like friend love? You love me like you want to kisssss me? You love me like a sister? You . . .

I drafted a long e-mail telling her that, yes, I loved her too, but not in the same way, but that I wouldn't let any of it affect our friendship and that I . . .

And then I just let it go. And phew! I did good there.

It turned out that "love" or "love you" is a common way to end an e-mail in the States.

I had no idea!

I still had a very French way of speaking, which I'm sure raised a lot of eyebrows when I first was assimilating into New York society. There was a whole new level of language to master.

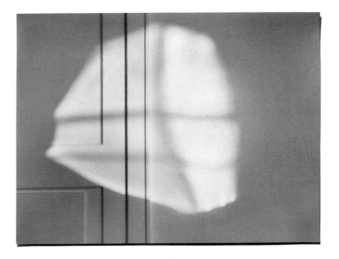

And just because you "love!" someone doesn't mean you necessarily want to have lunch with that person. Ah, just another example of the cultural gap between Paris and New York that I had to bridge. . . .

IN NEW YORK: "Oh my Gaaaaaad, so happy to see you! How aaaare you?"

IN PARIS: "Hey! How's it going?"

IN NEW YORK: Big hugs.

IN PARIS: You give kisses on the cheek. If you really want to show affection for someone, you give the cheek kisses with your hands on their shoulders. Wow. Best friends forever.

IN NEW YORK: "Your dress. OMG, I love it! Where did you find it???"

IN PARIS: "Your dress isn't bad (Not bad = *pas mal* = very French expression). Where'd you find it?"

IN NEW YORK: "Garance? She's my BEST friend!"

IN PARIS: "Garance? Yeah. I know her."

IN NEW YORK: "Beyoncé? She's hilarious!!!"

IN PARIS: "Beyoncé? Yeah, she's funny."

Voilà. Now you know another one of the secrets to Parisian coolitude, which is not to "love" anything too much. It's not really so bad, because when you say "I love you" in French, it carries a lot of weight.

And so if one day a Parisian comes up to you and says she "loves" your dress, I give you full permission to jump up and down and get the dress framed.

As for me, of course, I've adapted. I hug all the time, I love everyone, even my father, even my accountant ("Love . . ." Oops, I mean "Best!"), and I've come to find it all pretty fun. It's cute, this collective vocabulary euphoria.

I love it. ✗

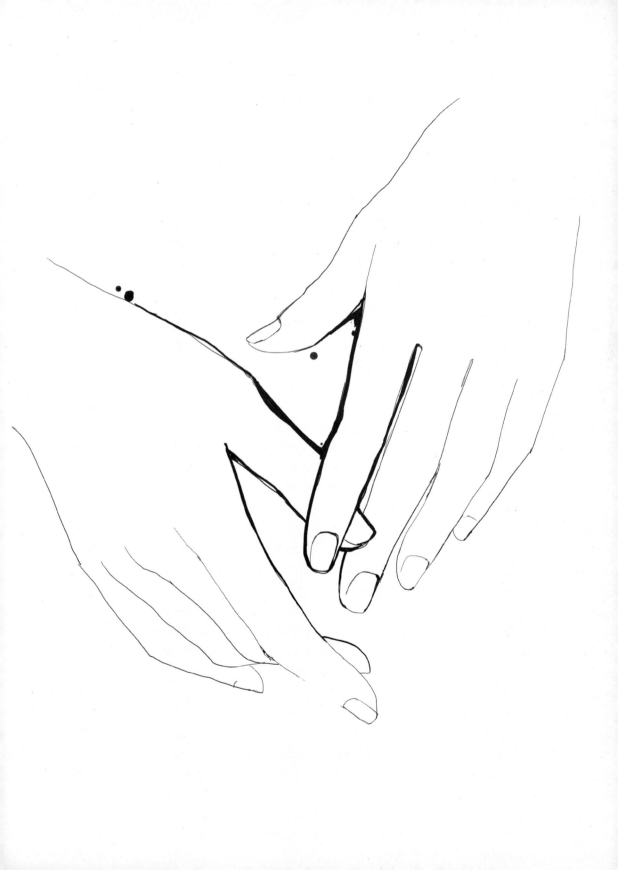

IN THE FAMILY

My family is *crazy*.

I'm pretty lucky, though. They're the right kind of crazy. Crazy, with a lot of love.

We all love each other so much, sometimes we can't help it—we judge, we're in each other's business, we drive each other nuts.

My family has taught me a lot about love, that it's possible to love someone who will . . .

TALK BEHIND YOUR BACK.

You know, the number-one rule of friendship, never talk behind someone's back? Doesn't apply to family. For some reason, in my family, our favorite sport is calling each other to complain about everyone's business.

So while my mother is talking to my sister about how I'll never settle down and don't take myself seriously enough ("No, but don't you think it's time for her to make a baby? I'm so worried!!!"), I'm talking to my brother about my mom's choices ("Why the hell doesn't she sell that house? Enough with the house drama!") and my sister is talking behind my dad's back ("Can you believe he didn't offer me a piece of his foie gras? Who does that?").

At first I thought we might be a dysfunctional family.

Now? I understand that these are words of love and care. As for our phone bills? Yeeeaahh.

Family will love you, but they will . . .

JUDGE YOUR LIFE CHOICES.

The bare minimum that you ask of anyone you know, from your friends to your mailman, is that they respect your life choices, right?

Yet, in my family, we all think we know better. Not that any one of us is more successful than the next: We've all been winners and losers at times.

Take that day I called my sister to tell her how broke and desperate I was. All I wanted was her shoulder to cry on. Yet here's what I heard:

"Listen, darling, that's your life choice, eh? You chose an artistic, boho life. Don't come complaining to me about not being able to even buy a pair of shoes.

"You made your choice: I buy shoes. You paint."

The shock! Okay, she was right. But the shock!!!

I still can't forget the sting of that remark . . . but time healed it.

Yep. Another thing I learned from my family? Loving is forgiving.

Because your family can love you and still . . .

THINK YOU'RE DATING A LOSER.

You think that because the guy is your choice, your family should accept him, right?

SURE.

They will give you the same look and plaster on that same fake smile as your friends did when you introduced your loser. They're going to talk behind your back ("How the hell did she find that guy? He's not even attractive!"), and when you break up with him three years later, after realizing that he actually was a loser, you'll never know if:

    1. You gave in to their influence.

    2. He was really a loser.

Same thing if they LOVE your boyfriend. Oh, the pressure. "He's great, keep him, don't do this, don't say that, don't break up, can we see him more"—aaaaaalll that.

Come on, family, get ahold of yourselves!

My advice: Protect your love story from your loving family until you're sure he's the one.

That's why, with family, sometimes it's best to . . .

PUT AN OCEAN BETWEEN YOU AND THEM.

I found that I love my family much better when we're apart.

From across an ocean, I can be everything to them that I could never be if I was living close.

× I can be generous with my time when I see them.

× I can be the Great Adviser (because I don't have my nose in their business, so they can call and tell me their story the way they see it and the distance helps me keep my opinion to myself).

× I can love them the way they are (because it's like watching a movie: From afar, all their little flaws are charming).

But, still, family will sometimes . . .

STOP TALKING TO YOU, EVEN THOUGH THEY MISS YOU DEARLY EVERY DAY.

In every family there comes a moment when the Worst Has Been Committed (this can range from saying hello in the wrong tone one morning to almost causing the whole family to go bankrupt).

In these instances, we stop talking. Sometimes it's just for a little while; sometimes it's two or three weeks. Sometimes it's for a few months, like last time my mom and my sister had a feud. It was not easy, as they live three minutes away from each other.

And, also, they were both calling me every day to see how the other was doing.

Till I put my foot down and told them they had to talk to each other 'cause I, in case they had forgotten, live an ocean away. (I do think they had forgotten. Modern communications!!!)

That said, we also have the tragic history of my dad and my granddad, whom I never met.

My granddad passed away a few years ago, and he hadn't spoken to my dad in over forty years, just because he hadn't agreed with his choice of marrying my mom. This is a very sad story.

Life is just too short to go to these extremes. Talk to each other, crazy people.

Your family can love you and still . . .

MAKE YOU LOSE ALL YOUR MONEY.

Each time this happened in my family, it began with very good intentions (including dreams of conquering the world).

Money is tricky, because it can really come between people. I've seen my family go bankrupt twice because of bad investments. But you learn that losing money is not the end of the world and that money actually comes back to you if you get back to work.

The bad news is that you might lose your home, your car, and your coffeemaker in the process.

And then have your neighbor buy them.

So, from observing my family over the years, here's what I've learned:

Don't lend money that you can't afford to never get back. Don't let anybody "take care of your money." Don't let anybody "take care of your business." Always sign a contract. Never ever think that a contract protects you from anything.

Don't believe the exceptions you hear about.

With all that knowledge, you should be able to enjoy the wonderful gifts of family:

Loving people with their flaws and their crazy quirks. Loving people who don't share their foie gras. Loving people with opposite political views. Loving people you've known all your life. Loving a brother. Loving a sister. Loving a half sister who is half your age and says crazy shit on Twitter.

Loving a mom and a dad, so much. And a stepdad. And the whole extended family. Loving it as your tiny family expands to become a whole tribe.

Loving it when your whole crazy family gets together. Getting older together. Rejoicing about the new generation ready to take over the world. Knowing your family better than you know yourself.

Always having a home to go back to when everything else falls apart. ✕

L'AMITIÉ

In France, we have *two words* to describe friendship.

Copain, which means a person you like and see casually from time to time.

And *ami,* the word that describes a person with whom a friendship runs deep.

To French people, *l'amitié* is like love, but it's even better.

Because it's rare and takes so long to build, it's incredibly precious.

And because you know that a true friend is every day and forever.

I have many *copains* and thousands of contacts in my phone. I could throw a party with a thousand people. With Internet, the circles have gotten bigger than ever. But friends I could call at four in the morning because I just broke up with my boyfriend?

I can count them on the fingers of one hand. And I am grateful I have that many.

TO ME, A TRUE FRIEND . . .

× . . . Doesn't judge you, but also has the right to disapprove of your full-body tattoo.

× . . . Will drop everything she's doing and come to your rescue if you have an emergency, but will also tell you when you're overreacting.

× . . . Has the right to be pissed at you when you overreact. But not for too long.

× . . . Doesn't make a move on your ex.

× . . . Doesn't make a move on your boyfriend!!!

× . . . Doesn't steal your friends!!! (Unless you encourage her to do so.)

× . . . Doesn't lie to you.

BEST THINGS TO DO WITH TRUE FRIENDS

× Just be yourself—the true essence of friendship.

× Travel to Greece and spend the whole time at the pool, chatting about life. A shame for Greece's beautiful landscapes, but such fun.

× Watch reruns of *Sex and the City* while chugging gelato.

× Wile away your entire day doing nothing, possibly ending up drunk at a bar at 2:00 a.m., and no one's to blame.

In my opinion, the international *crème de la crème* friend activity:

× The morning after a big night out, sipping tea and recapping all of the night's events.

THINGS YOU WANT A TRUE FRIEND TO BE ABLE TO SAY TO YOU

× "Yeah, okay, maybe you're right. You've gained a few. We'll stop our Ben & Jerry's couch parties for the next couple months."

× "You look stunning in that photo!"

× "That outfit just doesn't work on you."

× "I saw your man with another woman."

or

× "Your boyfriend is amazing. Stop making up stories; you're being paranoid."

SIGNS THAT IT'S A TRUE FRIENDSHIP

× You don't need to have a plan to get together. You can see each other with nothing on the agenda. You just know you want to spend time together, and you decide what you'll do after.

× Your friend is with people who are magnificently cooler or amazingly more important than you (yeah, it happens all the time in New York) and introduces you as if you're the greatest thing in the world.

× After three minutes of silence in a conversation, no one feels embarrassed.

× With a true friend, you can be completely yourself.

× You don't need to act like the cool girl who has "a ton of friends, a great job, and an awesome boyfriend, wahoooo!" You can just be you.

× Even after not seeing each other for a year, you feel like you're picking up a conversation you didn't quite finish the day before.

× After thirty-five years of friendship, you still laugh together like teenagers (my mom and her best friend, so awesome).

STUPID PROBLEMS THAT CAN KILL A FRIENDSHIP

× Jealousy: Jealousy stems from desire. If you hate someone because she has everything you want, remember that you probably started by loving her because of everything she has. Keep yourself in check.

× Money: In friendships, as in love, you have to be generous and let others be generous, even if it's just paying for coffee. You give what you can, whether in affection, money, intelligence, experience, contacts, or a great homemade lasagna.

× Distance: You have to pick up the phone. Call, Skype, text, whatever it is. I'm the worst at this, and sometimes I can't even get it together to respond to e-mails. So I never hold it against anyone if they can't call me, but friendships are a bit like flowers.

They suffer if you don't sing to them.

FRIENDSHIP RED FLAGS

× A social climber is a social climber. If he's social-climbing with others, he's social-climbing with you. You don't have to sever your friendship, as a social climber can be extremely entertaining. Just know what you're in for. Protect yourself.

× Unidirectional friendships—a more frequent problem than you think. Asking, "How are things for you?" (and then listening without checking your Twitter feed) should not be a sacrifice for a friend.

While deep friendships can sometimes be formed in three minutes, other superficial ones can linger on for years.

LIKE IN LOVE . . .

× You have to be able to get over a disagreement and even a big fight. Say you're sorry and let go.

× You have to be patient. Sometimes people have weird or difficult moments that can make you feel like they're not themselves and you're not in the picture.

Just wait for them. It can take months, but a real friend usually comes back.

AND LIKE IN LOVE . . .

× Some friendships die, but it doesn't mean they weren't beautiful and true. ✕

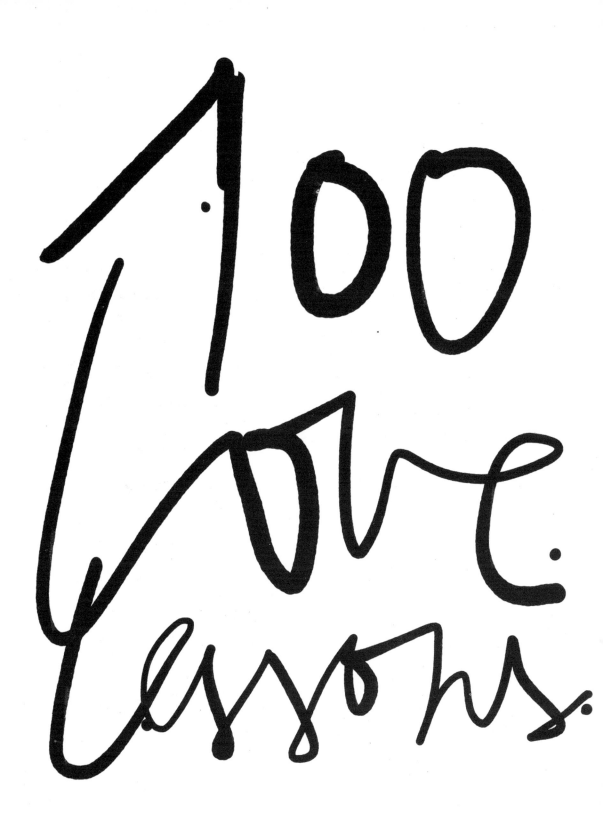

What's the saying? *You live, and you learn.*

I've learned something precious from every man (or woman) I've fallen for. Even when love didn't last more than a few days, even when it ended badly. I think about all these love stories (except one) with an incredibly fond heart. And I value each lesson they (most times inadvertently) taught me.

And even if I've maybe had a few more than I'm going to tell you about here, these are the nine loves that really changed me and taught me about life.

the first

I met my first boyfriend when I was fourteen. He was a skateboarder who traveled the world (with his parents; you can't be that cool at that age), and he was visiting Corsica.

I wrote his name on my jeans in what I thought was a very unique way to prove my affection.

But soon I realized he loved me more than I loved him. You'd think I would have basked in his devotion, but I didn't.

Too much love made me become terribly entitled and cruel. Maybe also I was just a dumb teenager who thought she knew about life.

I learned my first lesson in love:

1. IT'S FOOLISH TO BE FULL OF YOURSELF.

After three years of a pretty volcanic long-distance relationship, dramatic break-ups, and make-ups like only young lovers can do, I cheated on him. Technically, it was not cheating: I had broken up with him, only he wouldn't accept it, and he would be back, which leads me to the next lesson:

2. WHEN SOMEONE BREAKS UP WITH YOU, DON'T HANG IN THERE. GO AWAY!

the regretted

I was eighteen when I met a very handsome redheaded boy, sweet and fun and gentle. I fell passionately for him. The wonderful thing about him?

He made me discover great sex.

So great that twenty years later I still remember it. Ah, sigh, the lesson:

3. THE BEST IS NOT *ALWAYS* YET TO COME.

4. KEEP A GOOD SEX DIARY. TAKE PHOTOS. VIDEO? TOO RISKY? WRITE ABOUT IT. YOU MIGHT WANT TO REMEMBER HOW GOOD IT WAS, AT SOME LATER MOMENT IN YOUR LIFE.

5. JUST BECAUSE IT HAPPENS EARLY IN LIFE DOESN'T MEAN THAT IT DOESN'T COUNT.

But my first boyfriend didn't give up so fast. His passion was strong, and he had a plan. Our families went to the same place during the summer holidays, and he brought his ten best friends with him. I was naïve enough to think that our story was in the past and that his friends had become my friends.

All summer we hung out, and they did everything they could think of to come between my sweet love genius and me.

They talked down to him, ostracized him, mocked his hair color.

Now I know there is a word for what they did: They bullied him.

I was stupid and easily influenced. I didn't see. I went back to my first boyfriend. I still feel awful about the way it happened: I didn't stand up for him. I wish things had gone differently.

I left him, but I was the one who lost.

6. YOUR BOYFRIEND'S FRIENDS WILL MOST TIMES STAY WHAT THEY ARE: YOUR BOYFRIEND'S FRIENDS.

7. DON'T UNDERESTIMATE HOW FAR A MAN WILL GO TO GET YOU BACK.

8. DON'T STAND BY AND WATCH SOMEONE YOU CARE ABOUT GET HURT. YOU WILL NEVER FORGIVE YOURSELF.

the first

(YES, AGAIN)

So first boyfriend and I were back together, but you know the odds; this couldn't last for long. At that stage, I was with him for many stupid reasons, one of the worst being (shame on me) comfort. I was still living in Corsica; he had a nice apartment in Paris. That, and the fact that he just wouldn't let me go.

9. IN LOVE, AS WELL AS IN LIFE, COMFORT IS NEVER A GOOD REASON.

10. SOME PEOPLE WON'T LET YOU GO. IT DOESN'T MEAN YOU HAVE TO STAY.

Obviously, the familiarity turned to boredom. I became even more impossible with him; I didn't like anything about him anymore. I should have left, but what did I know? I was nineteen and clueless.

11. SOME LESSONS CAN'T BE TAUGHT. YOU HAVE TO EXPERIENCE THEM.

I stayed with him—waited and waited around. I didn't know what real love was. Maybe real love was knowing someone by heart and feeling comfortable with him even if you're a bit bored? I had no idea.

12. IF YOU'RE BORED AT NINETEEN, LEAVE.

I was so bored that one night I went to a club with a friend and lost my head for the first guy I saw.

the mistake

I hate, hate, hate this story and this man so much. This is one of those very scary stories that so many girls have but that none of us talk about.

I was lucky; nothing bad happened to me. But I want to talk about it so that if you ever end up in this situation, you will think about me and run.

Like a marathon session of *Homeland,* the whole thing happened over maybe six hours.

I was in a club, and I thought I was a grown woman, but in his eyes, I was probably very cute, fresh, and clueless—and possibly a little drunk too.

He was there with his friends. He was older and impressive, and girls were throwing themselves at him.

But he kept staring at me. I could feel his eyes undressing me. I was flattered that he would even notice me, set all his attention on me. We ended up sharing a drink, and he must have seduced me, because I decided to do like they do in the movies and tell my friends I was going home with him. We got into his car, ending up at his place.

As soon as we arrived, I felt trapped and guilty. It was obvious what this guy wanted, and it was even more obvious that he was interested in nothing else.

I suddenly was not drunk at all anymore: I had gotten myself into a very bad situation.

I was still trying to look cool, older than I was, and experienced, and I don't know where it would have gotten me if he hadn't disappeared for a second to go to the bathroom after trying to give me the most disgusting kiss of my life.

I saw my chance. I grabbed my stuff, and left as fast as I could, finding myself walking, completely lost, in the middle of the night. I was lucky I found my way home; I was lucky nothing bad happened to me during that long, terrible walk of shame and guilt that I will never forget.

I remember how it feels to be a teenager, to feel insecure and to want to belong to the world of adults. And I know what it feels like when older people put pressure on you.

It can go so wrong. In so many ways. And the worst?

No matter what people tell you, it's hard to shake that feeling of shame and guilt.

13. PROTECT YOURSELF. HAVE A SUPPORT SYSTEM, FRIENDS WHO WILL LOOK OUT FOR YOU.

14. PROTECT YOURSELF. YOUR BODY AND YOUR MIND ARE YOUR TREASURES. THERE ARE SO MANY OTHER WAYS TO PROVE YOU'RE COOL AND MATURE.

15. BY THE WAY, WE HAVE NOTHING TO PROVE TO ANYONE BUT OURSELVES.

16. PROTECT YOURSELF. TALK ABOUT THESE THINGS WHEN THEY HAPPEN. WHAT YOU HIDE WILL NEVER HEAL.

the smoke screen

I had moved to a small university town, Aix-en-Provence, to study.

My first boyfriend and I were still doing a sort of very, very long-distance relationship, which was helping us both ignore the fact that we would never be happy together.

Studying? Well, I was spending more time at rave parties than on academics. I was having so much fun.

I was spending more time partying than studying, out every night until dawn with my best friend, Anne. And that's how one night I met the most handsome, sexy, mysterious guy.

I don't remember how we first kissed; it must have been late. I couldn't put my finger on what made him so sexy and mysterious, but I couldn't get over it. After hanging out at a few parties together, we became boyfriend and girlfriend.

17. DON'T REMEMBER THE FIRST KISS? RED ALERT!

Days with him were pretty boring. I soon realized that he seemed mysterious because he actually had nothing very interesting to say. And no sense of humor, as you may have guessed—but, who knows why, I was hooked.

We would wake up late, he would smoke weed and I would pretend to smoke weed.

18. PRETENDING TO SMOKE WEED? RED ALERT!!

But night would always come and we'd go out and have fun again. I got sort of carried away by the alternative lifestyle (really, I'm much more of a day person) and was totally under the spell of his crazy green eyes. Not gonna brag about the sex here: Crazy party people and loads of weed doesn't often equal good sex.

19. AVERAGE SEX? RED ALERT!!!

Until one day, guess what happened?

He broke up with me.

Nobody had ever broken up with me. When he told me that things weren't working (what, really?), I thought I was going to DIE, capitals. I went back to my roommate, fell on the couch, cried my heart out, slept for two days and two nights.

I guess it was now time to repay my sleep debt.

When I woke up, I was over him. Wait. What?

20. NIGHT GUYS ARE AS UNREAL AS THEY SEEM.

21. WATCH FOR RED FLAGS. BEWARE OF FAKE LOVE STORIES.

22. IF YOU'RE BORED WITH HIM DURING THE DAY, IT JUST MEANS YOU'RE BORED.

23. EXHAUSTION WILL REALLY MESS WITH YOUR HEAD. THE CURE? GO TO BED! (ALONE, FOR ONCE!)

24. POTHEADS, REALLY?

the girl

Falling for really cute guys was starting to become a thing and apparently not such a good one, so for a change I fell for a very cute girl I met at a café on a long summer day.

We were friends at first and I loved everything about her, but still, I was pretty startled the day she grabbed me to plant a kiss on my lips. Here is what went through my mind during these very unanticipated seconds:

× What am I doing? Am I kissing a girl? Weird!!! Hey, it's not . . . bad? Wait, what's happening . . . Okay, let's kiss again? Just to see?

I was twenty-one and I was eager to explore. And these feelings and sensations were all so new. It was a bit scary and a lot amazing, but one thing I knew was: I had butterflies in my belly.

25. FOLLOW THE BUTTERFLIES.

26. NEVER SAY NEVER. LOVE WILL SURPRISE YOU. IT'S CALLED SELF DISCOVERY.

The funny thing is it got serious. We became a real couple. But it was complicated—it was hard to shift my self perception. And it was even harder to see the way some people—even close friends—distanced themselves. But I loved her. I wanted to be strong and proud and not succumb to the pressures of society.

27. OH, ALSO—ADVERSITY IS THE BEST FUEL FOR LOVE!

We loved each other for two years. But by the end I had realized that love is no different whether you're with a man or a woman. When it's good it's good, when it's bad it's bad. We had a great run. But then one day I fell head over heels for a man. Again.

28. IF YOU WANT TO KISS A GIRL, GO AHEAD, KISS A GIRL. SHE COULD BE THE LOVE OF YOUR LIFE. MAYBE SHE WON'T BE THE LOVE OF YOUR LIFE, AND THAT WILL BE OKAY TOO.

the real love

By now I was twenty-three and I was really into the music scene. One night, I was at a private concert in a friend's house. When I had the first and only coup de foudre *of my life (that's what we call it, in France, when love hits you like a bolt of lightning. Yes yes, we are romantic). Here's how it went.*

I saw him first. He didn't see me (turns out he's blind as a bat). He was playing the drums (I know, hot). I stood in the middle of the dance floor while everybody around me was dancing (I know, loser). When the concert ended and everybody had left, I was still standing there in the middle of the dance floor like the Statue of Liberty, looking at him. He said hi. I didn't answer; I was totally frozen. Oh wow.

Then he turned and kissed his girlfriend, who I couldn't really see in the dark room but who I pictured as the more beautiful younger sister of Daria Werbowy (I realized much later when I got a better look that she was not).

29. *COUP DE FOUDRE:* WILL MOST TIMES LIFT YOUR HEART AND THEN SMASH IT TO PIECES ON THE FLOOR.

30. DON'T IDEALIZE OTHER GIRLS. THEY ARE AS INSECURE AS YOU ARE.

The morning after, I called my mother.

I called my sister. I called my friends.

I told them I had met the man of my dreams (I was pretty emphatic and intense at twenty-three).

31. IT'S OKAY TO BELIEVE IN PRINCE CHARMING.

I was in love. In love like never before. Nothing would stop me. I knew he was with someone else and I didn't want to break them up, because I knew eventually the stars would align and we would be together. This might sound crazy, but I knew. I started putting everything in order in my mind, thinking of those long days I would have to wait by my window . . .

The next day, someone rang at my door.

It was the musician.

32. ALWAYS MAKE SURE YOUR DOORBELL IS WORKING.

33. TRY TO STAY CHIC AT HOME; YOU NEVER KNOW WHO MIGHT BE RINGING (SHE SAYS, TYPING AWAY AT HER LAPTOP IN HER OLDEST SWEATPANTS).

He said he had just come by to drop off some flyers for his next concert. The friends we had in common had given him my address. Okay! I'll take your flyers.

34. DON'T UNDERESTIMATE THE LENGTHS TO WHICH A GUY WILL GO TO SEE YOU.

35. DON'T UNDERESTIMATE THE POWER OF *NOT* CONNECTING THROUGH A PHONE.

I offered him a drink.

36. ALWAYS HAVE A DRINK TO OFFER.

He stayed all night.

37. ALWAYS BE READY TO GIVE UP YOUR PLANS FOR A NIGHT.

We talked.

38. NO SEX THE FIRST NIGHT, YOU CRAZY PEOPLE!!!

Here is what we talked about: Our lives. Where we came from. Our dreams. All the books we'd read. All the movies we'd seen. All the travels we'd done. And also . . .

He had a girlfriend. He had exams coming up. He was busy. But we had shared our lives and our dreams, and we decided that as soon as he was finished with his exams, in two months, we would leave together and hitch-hike around Europe.

I said okay; I renewed my passport and waited for July like the heroine of a romantic love story.

39. THERE IS ECSTASY IN ANTICIPATION. DON'T DEPRIVE YOURSELF OF IT.

40. SAY YES TO ROMANCE.

41. HITCHHIKE? YEAAAH . . . YOU DON'T HAVE TO TELL YOUR MOM *EVERYTHING.*

July came and I was ready. We still hadn't spoken since our crazy talking night. Of course I was stalking him a little bit, asking our friends about his comings and goings, but I was very careful to stay out of his way. Keep in mind, this was easy for me: I knew we were meant to be.

I just had to let fate do all the work.

42. IN SEDUCTION, SOMETIMES ABSENCE IS BETTER. GIVE SPACE, GIVE DISTANCE, DON'T CALL. TRUST THE PROCESS: IF IT'S MEANT TO BE, IT'LL COME TO YOU.

One night he had a concert that I went to. I talked with him after and he told me he was ready for our trip. We decided on a place to meet for the big departure. I was ready to explode I was so happy.

But.

Later that night, I saw him leave with his girlfriend, holding her hand.

I'm not joking.

43. GUYS? COMPLICATED.

Still, I had made my decision; I was leaving with him. We were just friends who had decided on a whim to hitchhike across Europe, right? I would go to meet him as planned, even if I was afraid he wouldn't show and was going to marry his girlfriend.

44. GIRLS? CRAZY.

He showed up! I didn't say a word about his girlfriend, and we left. We traveled through Nice, Milan, Venice, Vienna, and Prague. The most beautiful cities in the world. I could write a book about it if I wasn't already writing a book. We had our first passionate kiss one week into the trip, in the cabin of an old republic train, as we rode through a thunderstorm.

It was so romantic and so sensual.
He became my everything.

Oh, he had broken up with his girlfriend before we had left, by the way. I would later learn that they had been on and off for a while. He was a good, honest man.

45. GOOD, HONEST GUYS, LIKE IN MOVIES? THEY REALLY EXIST.

46. TRUE, BEAUTIFUL ROMANCE, LIKE IN MOVIES? IT REALLY EXISTS.

When we got back to the South of France, I moved in with him. We were so in love. He was incredibly fun and talented. My mom loved him. I loved his mom. He was a great lover. It was all just too much to take. I went from being crazy in love to just being plain crazy.

I started living only for him. Forgetting my friends. Waiting around for him. Acting jealous. Stalking him. Crying on the carpet because he was going for a coffee with a friend and I was not invited.

What was wrong with me?

47. ATTENTION: YOU ARE ENTERING CRAZY LOVE ADDICTION TERRITORY. IT WILL MAKE YOU STUPID, UGLY. YOU WILL SAY THAT IT'S ALL IN THE NAME OF LOVE—BUT REALLY IT'S ALL ABOUT YOU AND YOUR NEEDS. WHAT YOU WANT IS TO POSSESS. DON'T GO THERE. IF YOU START GOING THERE, SLAP YOURSELF. OR COME SEE ME; I WILL SLAP YOU.

He left me.

Best idea he's ever had.

He broke up with the shipwreck of a love mess that I was. He told me to leave, which I refused to do. After two days (with both of us in his apartment crying and shouting) of emotional blackmail and me hiding the front-door keys (yes, hiding the front-door keys) so he couldn't throw me out, a friend of a friend called me for a random reason.

And when she heard my voice, she decided she had to come get me.

48. EVEN IF THE WORLD AS YOU KNOW IT IS ENDING, ANSWER YOUR PHONE.

I spent the next twenty days on the couch of that girl I didn't even really know. She would become one of my best friends, but I couldn't have cared less at that moment. I had lost my reason to live. I couldn't breathe, I couldn't eat, I couldn't talk about anything other than him. I could only smoke and cry. She let me cry.

49. OPEN YOURSELF TO BEING HELPED. A STRANGER MAY SAVE YOU.

I cried until I had no tears left, and then I cried without tears for days. My heart felt completely bruised, as if someone had trampled on it. I felt broken inside and out. Everything was gray. All the colors were gone. Oh, so that's why they call it a heartbreak!

50. YOU CAN'T KNOW A HEART-BREAK UNTIL YOU HAVE ONE.

But one day I was out of cigarettes. I had to go out and get more. I threw on whatever I found on the floor and went outside. I felt the fresh air on my cheeks. I started looking around. I felt the world around me, people coming and going. Outside, life was continuing.

The colors started to come back.

At that moment, I knew I was going to survive.

51. HEARTBREAKS ARE MISERABLE. BE NICE TO HEARTBROKEN PEOPLE.

52. YOU WILL SURVIVE.

53. KNOWING THAT YOU WILL SURVIVE WILL CHANGE YOU FOREVER. I WISH A GOOD HEARTBREAK TO ANYONE.

After that specific moment, I started feeling better. I understood that even though I still loved him, I would be able to live without him and could even be happy without him. One day, I would most certainly forget him.

54. SOMETIMES, ONLY TIME CAN HEAL YOUR WOUNDS. JUST TRUST THAT IT WILL.

That's when he came back.

55. SOMETIMES, A BREAKUP CAN SAVE A RELATIONSHIP.

We got back together. I swore I would never go back to crazy. No more drama. I swore I would respect him and his life. And I did. I stopped being petty and possessive, and that became my new rule for relationships.

This was one of the most important lessons of my life.

Thanks to him, I became a much, much better person, and not just in love but in life.

56. LOVING SOMEONE IS NOT OWNING THEM.

57. BOUNDARIES: RESPECT, NO SWEARING, NEVER TREATING SOMEONE LIKE THEY BELONG TO YOU. HE TAUGHT ME ALL THAT.

58. IT'S NOT ALWAYS ABOUT BEING RIGHT. SOMETIMES THE MOMENT IS FOR LISTENING, GIVING IN, CHANGING.

59. GIVING SOMEONE THE STRENGTH TO CHANGE IS ONE OF THE GREAT POWERS OF REAL LOVE.

We lived happily ever after . . . for a few years. Unfortunately, we were so young when we met. We changed. Our life goals changed, and one day we realized we were unhappy.

But our love was so strong that we kept trying for one more year. Long enough for me to know it really wasn't working anymore. But still I couldn't leave him. I was too attached.

I was twenty-six, and I knew I had to break up with the man I'd believed was the one, the real one, the only one, my fairy tale. I couldn't bear the idea. We kept trying . . .

And then one day I met a man AT A PARTY. Should have seen the red lights right there, don't you think?

60. SOME LESSONS HAVE TO BE LEARNED TWICE.

the limbo

By this time I was in Marseille, working my first job in film. We were giving a big party one night, and that's where I saw him. He was so handsome, I couldn't believe it (Oh, no! Again!!!). But he was also . . . Wait. He was mostly just handsome. Very kind, but a little bit young, a little bit . . . Not the smartest, I decided.

Still, because I was in a tough moment of my life, and because this time I was sure it was safe and I was in control, I decided to go home with him in order to . . .

Have the first real one-night stand of my life.

I was twenty-six! I had never had a good one-night stand! My friends were having one-night stands! Why shouldn't I!!?

And, to this day, I still still haven't.

The one-night stand: I've heard it exists; I even know some friends who've had one. It just has never happened *to me*.

I stayed at his place that night. And the night after. My one-night stand turned into a two-night stand, and then three, and then four. And, like that, in a very French manner, we were boyfriend and girlfriend. A few nights later, I decided to get my life together (remember, I was still living with my musician) and move in with my best friends.

I had found the courage (where I could) to leave my love, fully aware that I was, again, jumping from one relationship to the next.

61. SOME GIRLS ARE JUST NOT CUT OUT FOR ONE-NIGHT STANDS.

62. SOME GIRLS ARE JUST AFRAID TO BE ALONE.

63. DON'T BE ONE OF THESE GIRLS.

64. SIDE NOTE: LIVING WITH YOUR BEST FRIENDS IS THE COOLEST THING YOU WILL EVER DO.

My weird story continued. I thought of him as a rebound to get me over my long-overdue breakup. It's nice to have a boy toy. It's fun, uncomplicated, sexy.

65. FOR THE RECORD, THIS IS HOW A RELATIONSHIP IS SUPPOSED TO BE: FUN, UNCOMPLICATED, AND SEXY.

It started to get more serious, though still in a lighthearted way. I was feeling protected, in a sort of life bubble. After a while, I moved in with him. We were living together. We were official. I loved him, without having even been in love with him. But, slowly, the sexy left. Then the fun left. Then one day the uncomplicated left, and suddenly I woke up, broke up, and looked back with terrible angst: I had stayed for three years in love limbo.

66. IF A RELATIONSHIP FEELS MORE LIKE A COZY BLANKET THAN IT FEELS LIKE A RELATIONSHIP, RUN AWAY.

That's what I did, I ran, even though I was thirty by that time and worried that I would never find anybody to love me again.

67. YOU CAN'T GO AROUND THINKING STUPID THINGS LIKE THAT.

68. IT'S NEVER TOO LATE FOR LOVE!

I moved to Paris. I decided it was time to be single! To experience what being thirty had to offer! Let's have fun and travel with single friends! Let's be selfish! Let's. Have. Fuuuuuun!!!

Wooooooohoooooooo . . .

Ooooooaaand I met another guy.

the unloved

He was Parisian. I told him I hated Parisians, because they're pretentious, unreliable, and mostly annoying. We fought a little bit about that. But he was also so cute in his skinny jeans that I thought I would give him a try.

It was by now high time to get rid of my cuteness obsession. I was worse than a modelizer! I was worse than my Parisian himself!!!

Oops, nope! I actually wasn't. After a few weeks of a very Parisian romance, lots of cafés, some cigarettes, a bit of baguette (eheheheheh), and many French kisses, I realized we were three in that relationship: him, me, and his phone. He was pretty obsessed with it. My instinct told me it was not just Angry Birds.

So, one day, I decided to just go ahead and check it.

69. ONE OF THE MOST IMPORTANT THINGS IN LOVE IS TO RESPECT THE OTHER PERSON'S PRIVACY. DO NOT CHECK THEIR PHONE. DO NOT CHECK THEIR WALLET. DO NOT CHECK THEIR DRAWERS. GIVE THEM YOUR TRUST AND RESPECT.

70. EXCEPT WHEN YOUR INSTINCTS GO CRAZY. (IT'S LIKE THAT. IT'S A GIRLS' RULE.)

Yes, I did it reluctantly, but I checked his phone. Doubts confirmed: He was cheating on me.

It was the first time this had happened to me. Weirdly, I didn't care so much about the other girl. Or girls. Remember lesson #30? I had learned not to idealize the other girl. But it immediately made me realize something about our relationship: As vexed as I was, I didn't care enough about him to really suffer over his treachery.

Had I been in love, I might have tried to understand the situation, the why, the how, and if I was able to forgive. But in this case, it just made me want to go far, far away.

71. CHEATING IS OFTEN THE SYMPTOM OF A PROBLEM.

72. EACH CASE IS SPECIAL, BUT ONE THING IS ALWAYS TRUE: IT DEEPLY HURTS.

73. DON'T BE A CHEATER.

I hit him with my bag a few times for good measure and left.

It was now time for me to be single. No, really, I was ready. I didn't even need the party, the wooooooohoooo, and I had given up on my idea of a nice, simple, and sexy one-night stand. It was time to be on my own and enjoy my life and my work and my friends and myself.

This was going to be good.

And just as I was saying all that, of course, you know what happened.

74. UNDERSTAND YOUR PATTERNS.

I met someone.

the kindred spirit

His name was Scott.

I met him taking photos at Fashion Week, and we became friends.

Scott made me laugh. He had beautiful eyes. He was terribly smart. He was an incredibly talented photographer. Super gentle. A bit moody. He was very American. I was very French.

I would see him when he came to Paris for Fashion Week. At first we were just friends. We would chat and fight for hours about life and photography and fashion. We had

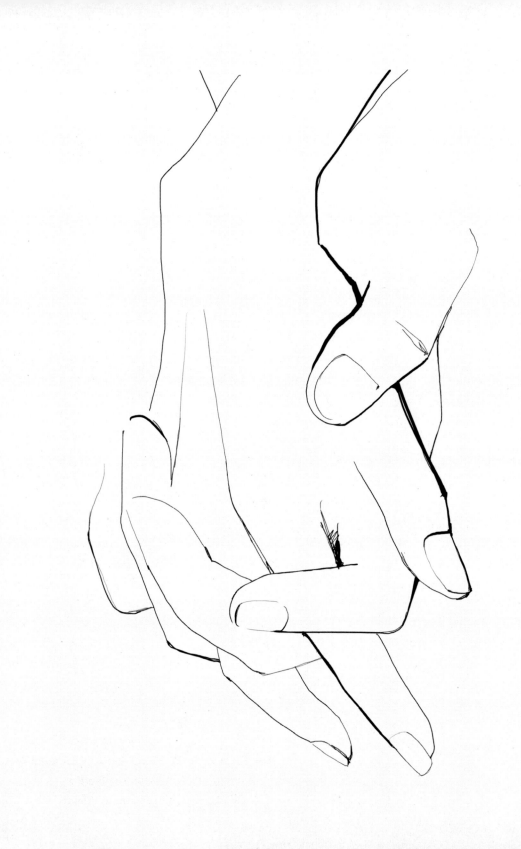

opposite views on everything, from politics to the taste of coffee. I'd never had a friend like that.

75. LIFE WILL SEND UNEXPECTED PEOPLE YOUR WAY.

76. DON'T REJECT SOMEONE BECAUSE YOU DIDN'T EXPECT THEM.

77. SOMETIMES OPPOSITES ATTRACT.

He was married and I wanted to be single. Perfect! It was just a friendship.

78. EXCEPT THAT FACTS DON'T PROTECT US FROM EMOTIONS.

The thing is, we laughed a lot. He was funny and self-deprecating—my favorite trait in a man.

79. A SENSE OF HUMOR IS THE WAY TO A WOMAN'S HEART (OKAY, TO MY HEART).

But one day, as he was about to fly back to New York, something happened. We said our goodbyes and hugged like Americans do, he gave me an undefinable look, and then he walked away. I watched him disappear into the distance . . .

At that moment my heart ripped apart. I had never felt anything like it. I started to cry. I had no idea why.

80. WHEN IN DOUBT, GO SEE YOUR FRIENDS.

I called my best friend. We talked for hours about this weirdly emotional friendship.

She said, "Seriously? Can't you see you are in love?"

81. SOMETIMES, REASON SCRAMBLES WHAT YOUR HEART IS TELLING YOU.

I explained to her again how impossible all this was.

He was not for me. We were too different; it was too complicated.

She answered: "You don't decide who you fall in love with."

82. LOVE MAKES YOU FORGET EVERYTHING YOU THOUGHT YOU KNEW ABOUT LOVE.

I went back home, heartbroken. So that was it. I was in love. And my love had just left Paris.

In a way it was a relief. Nothing could happen. And I needed time to process.

But I was aching and I couldn't stop thinking about him. I sent him an e-mail to say goodbye, telling him how sad I was that he had to leave.

The thing is, at that time, no one in Paris had e-mail on their phones. I had imagined he would get my message once he was back home.

But Scott was from New York, and he had a Blackberry. He got my e-mail on his way to the airport.

83. NEVER UNDERESTIMATE TECHNOLOGY.

He told the driver to turn around and go right back to Paris.

84. DON'T THINK THAT DISTANCE OR THE MEDIUM (AN E-MAIL) MAKE YOUR ACTIONS ANY LESS MEANINGFUL.

85. ROMANTIC SHOWS OF LOVE WILL MELT A WOMAN'S HEART

We met, and finally talked about our feelings. There was a lot of crying.

After that, there was no way to know what was going to happen.

I gave it a lot of thought. Talked it out for hours with my friends and my family. With my therapist. And then I decided to follow my heart.

86. THE ONLY REAL WAY TO LOVE IS TO GIVE YOUR HEART TO SOMEONE. TAKE DOWN THE SHIELD; RELINQUISH CONTROL AND LET GO OF THE FEAR.

I knew I would probably get hurt, and I knew that I couldn't be responsible for his life.

That's exactly what I told him. We would wait. He had to make up his mind and work his life out on his own.

87. GIVING YOUR HEART DOESN'T MEAN LOSING YOUR MIND.

88. SOME THINGS TAKE TIME. YOU CAN'T MAKE EVERYTHING PERFECT IN AN INSTANT.

Months went by. Even if I had terrible moments of doubt, I was enjoying my almost-single life.

The relationship was sort of a beautiful distant dream.

89. REVEL IN EACH STAGE OF LOVE. FIRSTS ONLY HAPPEN ONCE. SAVOR THEM.

Then, slowly, things started to happen. After months of being apart, our relationship became a reality. For a while we continued the long distance, with me in Paris, him in New York . . .

But living apart gets old. I had wanted to live in New York City for such a long time. Still, I waited until the timing was right, and one day, it was suddenly all possible. I moved to New York.

What a wonderful time that was. He was beginning again, and our life together was taking shape. We moved in together and were incredibly happy, for what I thought would be forever.

But forever it was not. After a few great years, our connection slowly crumbled. Our passionate conversations became fights. Our funny differences became gaps we weren't able to bridge.

We kept holding on to our dream, but the reality was that we were miserable.

90. DREAMS ARE STRONG.

91. REALITY IS STRONGER.

As for me, I was getting older and thinking of starting a family.

The time should have been right to take that step together, and even if we thought we really wanted it, nothing was working the way it should have. Travels would keep us apart for weeks at a time. Fights would leave us angry and depleted. Looking back, I understand that we were not at the same place in our lives.

92. IN LOVE, TIMING IS OF THE ESSENCE.

I couldn't imagine having a baby in that environment, yet it was incredibly scary to think of leaving, of starting over, of being alone, with that dream of a family reduced to pieces.

I was terribly sad inside and trying to hold on to my old idea of our relationship.

93. WHEN IT'S REAL LOVE, GIVE IT ALL YOU HAVE.

We're so good at telling ourselves stories. It's all going to work out! He's a good man; I'm a good woman. So what if the connection is lost? Every couple goes through phases! Let's go to therapy!!! Let's make. It. Work.

94. UNTIL YOU CAN'T ANYMORE.

I guess things had started to change inside me. I began seeing life differently. Enjoying my time alone. My friends, my family, would tell me how relaxed I was when I was on my own. It's not that we didn't love each other anymore. It's just that, for reasons that will probably take me years to really understand, we were no longer happy together.

95. ALONE IS BETTER THAN SAD AND UNHAPPY TOGETHER.

I also looked around me and saw the different ways that life can take shape. Different ideas of what family means. I saw some single friends happily having kids on their own. Possibilities started to form in my mind.

96. THERE ARE SO MANY PATHS. ALL OF THEM ARE RIGHT.

At this point, I was not even imagining meeting someone else. It's not my thing to actively look, and the idea of dating in New York gave me terrible chills. I knew one thing. If I was to leave Scott, I had to prepare myself to be on my own.

And, slowly, the idea started making me happy.

And the happy grew inside me, on the ashes of my moribund relationship.

And one day, I called Scott. He was away. We talked. We cried. We agreed. It was over.

97. BREAKUPS CAN BE MOMENTS OF GREAT UNDERSTANDING AND SURRENDER.

98. EVEN IN THE SADDEST MOMENTS, RESPECT IS THE MOST IMPORTANT THING.

I was so scared and so relieved at the same time. I remember telling my mom: "Mom, this is probably the most courageous thing I've ever done in my life." And it was.

More than my risky career choices or moving away from my home country.

This was a deeper kind of courage—the courage to keep looking for happiness, refusing to settle if it was not right. The courage to take a leap of faith, trusting that life would bring me everything I needed, however unscripted and unexpected my next chapter would be.

99. DON'T BE AFRAID.

It was a real act of self-love and self-trust. And it was my most valuable love lesson . . .

100. LOVE YOURSELF.

And I've never been happier. I'm thankful every day, as I walk through the streets of New York, alone, smiling, unafraid. My life is filled with friends, works of love, and possibilities, endless possibilities. I've never felt so wise, and I've never felt so young. I know I can make anything happen.

Oh, and I met someone the other day. . . .

And that will probably be a new chapter with so many new love lessons. I hope it will last forever, but maybe it will be just a few days, and it will be great either way. Because you never stop learning about love. Love is joy, pain, surrender, laughter, pleasure. Love is chemistry. Love is one of life's greatest adventures.

And with love, we're kids forever, stumbling and learning as life unfolds. And this is why, whatever happens, we must keep our hearts open. ✕

CONCLUSION

One more chapter, where I talk to you about my sex life,
was going to go here (with illustrations!!!).

But I thought it might be best to save for the next book.

Big kiss!

Garance

ACKNOWLEDGMENTS

This is that crazy page where you're allowed to thank everyone in your life. Where do you start? Where do you stop?

I'm just going to freestyle it. I want to say thank you . . .

To my team: You guys are the most amazing gift, and without you, this book could never have come together. My life would be a disaster.

To Erik Melvin and Brie Welch: Your support and your friendship mean the world to me.

To Emily Note, my closest collaborator, my friend, and also basically my boss: I don't know how to begin to tell you how you've made my life so much better, cooler, more exciting, and more fulfilling. I hope for many more years to come. And I hope I can in turn help you make your life everything you want it to be.

To my photo agents, Walter Schupfer and Delphine Del Val: Your amazing and powerful support means the world. Delphine, thank you for being a person with the most wonderful, warm heart. And also for being such a badass agent!

To Jessica Sindler, my editor, so patient and talented and understanding: Thank you.

Thank you to Julie Grau, Greg Mollica and the whole team at Spiegel & Grau for choosing me and for making me feel at home.

To Claudia Ballard and Tracy Fisher, my agents at WME, for the amazing support and for taking me so seriously. I guess someone needs to do that job, and that was always you!

Elina Asanti, you made my graphic dreams come true! Thank you for your kindness and your talent.

I also want to thank my friends who have helped me so much with this book: Jenna Lyons, Emmanuelle Alt, Diane von Furstenberg, Drew Barrymore, Lauren Cohan, Carole Benazet, Lauren Bastide, Courtney Crangi, Scott Schuman, and Ferdinando Verderi, thank you.

To Meyre Pepe: Please never leave me.

Chris Norton, thank you.

To all the wonderful men and women who have let me take their photos and have trusted me all through the years: Thank you.

To the readers of garancedore.com: You guys changed my life. Thank you forever!!!

And to my family. I love you.

ABOUT THE AUTHOR

Called the "guardian of all style" by *The New York Times*, GARANCE DORÉ is a photographer, illustrator, author, and founder of an eponymous influential style blog. Winner of the CFDA Eugenia Sheppard Media Award, Doré has contributed both as a writer and photographer to publications including American, British, and Paris *Vogue*, *The Wall Street Journal*, *The New York Times*, *T Magazine*, *Elle*, *The Guardian*, and *New York* magazine. She has collaborated with clients including Céline, Chloé, Chopard, Dior, Estée Lauder, J.Crew, L'Oréal, Louis Vuitton, Prada, NARS, and Tiffany & Co. In 2014 she launched her namesake brand with a line of stationery and paper goods. Originally from Corsica, she currently resides in New York City.

garancedore.com

Facebook.com/GaranceDoreOfficial

Instagram, Twitter, and Snapchat: @garancedore